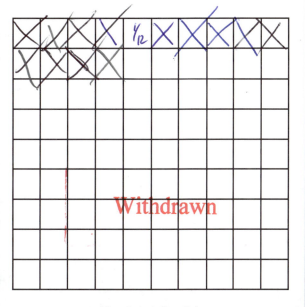

CUNARD

THE MOST FAMOUS OCEAN LINERS IN THE WORLD ™

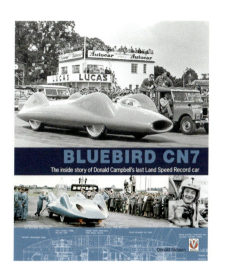

BLUEBIRD CN7

The inside story of Donald Campbell's last Land Speed Record car

Donald Stevens

Other great books from Veloce –

Speedpro Series

4-cylinder Engine – How to Blueprint & Build a Short Block For High Performance (Hammill)
Camshafts – How to Choose & Time Them For Maximum Power (Hammill)
Competition Car Datalogging Manual, The (Templeman)
Cylinder Heads – How to Build, Modify & Power Tune Updated & Revised Edition (Burgess & Gollan)
Distributor-type Ignition Systems – How to Build & Power Tune New 3rd Edition (Hammill)
Fast Road Car – How to Plan and Build Revised & Updated Colour New Edition (Stapleton)
Holley Carburetors – How to Build & Power Tune Revised & Updated Edition (Hammill)
Motorsport – Getting Started in (Collins)
Nitrous Oxide High-performance Manual, The (Langfield)
Speed secrets – Today's techniques for 4-stroke engine blueprinting & tuning (Swager)
Sportscar & Kitcar Suspension & Brakes – How to Build & Modify Revised 3rd Edition (Hammill)
SU Carburettor High-performance Manual (Hammill)
V8 Engine – How to Build a Short Block For High Performance (Hammill)
Weber DCOE, & Dellorto DHLA Carburetors – How to Build & Power Tune 3rd Edition (Hammill)

Those Were The Days ... Series

Alpine Trials & Rallies 1910-1973 (Pfundner)
Anglo-American Cars from the 1930s to the 1970s (Mort)
Hot Rod & Stock Car Racing in Britain in the 1980s (Neil)
MG's Abingdon Factory (Moylan)
Superprix – The Story of Birmingham Motor Race (Page & Collins)

General

Alpine & Renault – The Development of the Revolutionary Turbo F1 Car 1968 to 1979 (Smith)
Alpine & Renault – The Sports Prototypes 1963 to 1969 (Smith)
Alpine & Renault – The Sports Prototypes 1973 to 1978 (Smith)
Anatomy of the Works Minis (Moylan)
André Lefebvre, and the cars he created at Voisin and Citroën (Beck)
Art Deco and British Car Design (Down)
Autodrome (Collins & Ireland)
Autodrome 2 (Collins & Ireland)
Bentley Continental, Corniche and Azure (Bennett)
Bentley MkVI, Rolls-Royce Silver Wraith, Dawn & Cloud/Bentley R & S-Series (Nutland)
BMC Competitions Department Secrets (Turner, Chambers & Browning)
British at Indianapolis, The (Wagstaff)
British Cars, The Complete Catalogue of, 1895-1975 (Culshaw & Horrobin)
BRM – A Mechanic's Tale (Salmon)
Concept Cars, How to illustrate and design (Dewey)
Daily Mirror World Cup Rally 40, The (Robson)
Drive on the Wild Side, A – 20 Extreme Driving Adventures From Around the World (Weaver)
Fast Ladies – Female Racing Drivers 1888 to 1970 (Bouzanquet)
GT – The World's Best GT Cars 1953-73 (Dawson)
Honda NSX (Long)
Intermeccanica – The Story of the Prancing Bull (McCredie & Reisner)
Jack Sears, The Official Biography of – Gentleman Jaguar, The Rise of (Price)
John Chatham – 'Mr Big Healey' – The Official Biography (Burr)
Lamborghini Miura Bible, The (Sackey)
Montlhéry, The Story of the Paris Autodrome (Boddy)
Morris Minor, 60 Years on the Road (Newell)
Motor Racing – Reflections of a Lost Era (Carter)
Motorsport In colour, 1950s (Wainwright)
Nissan GT-R Supercar: Born to race (Gorodji)
Peking to Paris 2007 (Young)
RX-7 – Mazda's Rotary Engine Sportscar (Updated & Revised New Edition) (Long)
Speedway – Auto racing's ghost tracks (Collins & Ireland)
Supercar, How to Build your own (Thompson)
Tales from the Toolbox (Oliver)
Taxi! The Story of the 'London' Taxicab (Bobbitt)
Toleman Story, The (Hilton)
Triumph Bonneville!, Save the – The inside story of the Meriden Workers' Co-op (Rosamond)

From Veloce Publishing's new imprints:

Battle Cry! imprint

Soviet General & field rank officer uniforms: 1955 to 1991 (Streather)
Soviet military and paramilitary services: female uniforms 1941-1991 (Streather)

Hubble & Hattie imprint

Complete Dog Massage Manual, The – Gentle Dog Care (Robertson)
Dinner with Rover (Paton-Ayre)
Know Your Dog – The guide to a beautiful relationship (Birmelin)
My dog is blind – but lives life to the full! (Horsky)
Smellorama – nose games for your dog (Theby)
Waggy Tails & Wheelchairs (Epp)
Winston ... the dog who changed my life (Klute)
You and Your Border Terrier – The Essential Guide (Alderton)
You and Your Cockapoo – The Essential Guide (Alderton)

www.veloce.co.uk

First published in April 2010 by Veloce Publishing Limited, Veloce House, Parkway Farm Business Park, Middle Farm Way, Poundbury, Dorchester, Dorset, DT1 3AR, England.
Fax 01305 250479/e-mail info@veloce.co.uk/web www.veloce.co.uk or www.velocebooks.com.
ISBN: 978-1-84584-280-2 UPC: 6-368470-4280-6

Readers with ideas for automotive books, or books on other transport or related hobby subjects, are invited to write to the editorial director of Veloce Publishing at the above address.
British Library Cataloguing in Publication Data – A catalogue record for this book is available from the British Library. Typesetting, design and page make-up all by Veloce Publishing Ltd on Apple Mac.
Printed in India by Replika Press.

BLUEBIRD CN7

The inside story of Donald Campbell's last Land Speed Record car

GEARBOX SUSPENSION ARMS.

PROTEUS GAS TURBINE ENGINE
DELIVERING 4100 S.H.P. AT 11,000 R.P.M.
MODIFIED TO DRIVE FROM BOTH ENDS.

LIFTING JACKS.

RECIRCULATING BALL STEERING
NUT WITH DUAL CHAIN DRIVE.

HIGH TENSILE STEEL
WELDED HUB.

ENGINE FRONT DRIVE WITH
FREE WHEEL DEVICE.

REAR GEARBOX OIL TANK.

VER'S INSTRUMENT PANEL

BRAKE SYSTEM CHARGING AND
JACKING CONTROL PANEL.

VELOCE PUBLISHING
THE PUBLISHER OF FINE AUTOMOTIVE BOOKS

Designed
NORRIS

Contents

Acknowledgements

The intention behind this book is to right a great omission in the history of land speed record-breaking, and to pay respect to the dedication of two men in particular, Ken and Lew Norris, whose contribution to the image of British engineering has never been officially recognised. It is to them that I owe a debt of gratitude for the opportunity to participate in the 'Bluebird' and other ground-breaking projects undertaken by their company. Thanks also to Mike (the Squirrel) Varndell who encouraged me to start writing, and provided many other pieces of information from his fantastic collection of Campbell memorabilia. Grateful thanks are also due to British Petroleum Ltd, Rubery Owen Holdings Ltd, Goodyear Dunlop Ltd, Hexel Composites Ltd (ex-CIBA ARL), TRW Automotive Ltd (ex-Lucas-Girling), Federal Mogul Ltd (ex-Ferrodo), Rolls-Royce Heritage (Bristol-Siddeley Engines), The Bluebird Trust, and Geoff Hallawell, for their kind permission to use copyright photographs and data.

My lack of computer skills was compensated for by my great nephew, Nic Bowker, and James Haslam, both qualified aeronautical engineers, and by Nick Chapman, who between them respectively produced drawings, graphs, and cleaned up old slides. Thanks are also due to my good friends Phil Evemy and Sue Robinson for their encouragement and guidance in the book's preparation, and to my partner Jenny who calmed me down when computer 'malfunctions' made me want to drop the project.

Donald Stevens

Foreword

By Wing Commander Andy Green – OBE, MA, RAF – current
holder of the World Land Speed Record, and selected driver for
the 'Bloodhound' 1000mph (1609kph) car project

To this day, the World Land Speed Record remains the most challenging and exciting form of motor sport on earth. Uniquely, it features almost no design restrictions and has a single, simple aim – to produce a car faster than any other in history. British engineers have been extraordinarily successful in achieving this aim, and Britain has held this ultimate motoring prize for 68 of the Record's 111 year history. In detailing the remarkable story of the Bluebird CN7 in this book, Donald Stevens has captured the magic of this success.

The CN7 was quite literally 50 years ahead of its time, featuring a composite chassis, a data-logging system, and a sophisticated head-up display, technology that would be admired today in a land speed record car. The CN7's performance was also half a century ahead of its rivals, with a projected maximum (which I fully believe) of well over 450mph – and with the current wheel-driven record standing at only 458mph, the CN7 could break that today, given the chance.

It is perhaps ironic that the Norris brothers looked ahead to a supersonic rocket car, the CN8. Fifty years later, we are building just such a car, the Bluebird SSC, with the aim of inspiring a new generation of engineers and scientists in Britain – a new generation to follow in the footsteps of Donald Stevens and the Norris brothers. The remarkable story of the CN7 is a reminder of just how

Wing Commander Andy Green and Thrust SSC.
(Jeremy Davey/Thrust SSC)

good British engineering was, is, and will continue to be in the future; if we want it enough. Enjoy the fascinating tale that follows, in the knowledge that the skills and inspiration remain as relevant today as they were then.

Andy Green

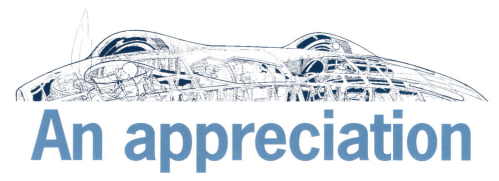

An appreciation

By Lew Norris, co-chief designer of Donald Campbell's 'Bluebirds,' the K7 hydroplane that broke the world water speed record seven times, and the Campbell-Norris 7 (CN7) land speed record breaker

"I was pleased to be asked to write a few words about Donald Stevens, who was our first employee in the newly formed company, Norris Brothers Limited, in 1954, based in Haywards Heath.

My memories are that, although young at the time, he was an excellent and very fine design draughtsman, and quickly became a valued member of our design team. He made a considerable contribution during the design of both the Water Speed Record boat and the Land Speed Record car, amongst other projects.

His enthusiasm and dedication to detail in every project he was involved in for us made him extra special – his book proves this."

The author and Lew Norris with the Campell-Norris 7 at the National Motor Museum. (Author's Collection)

Introduction

Since the dawn of the motoring age, the land speed record has fascinated a great many people. From the late 1800s to the late 1950s any attempt to break it brought international interest, and one of the greatest names in that period was that of Campbell; firstly Malcolm (later Sir Malcolm) and then Donald, his son.

In 1937, *Speed* magazine published an article by WB Killen BSc entitled 'The Ultimate Land Speed Record.' This article deduced, by means of graphs, that the ultimate record would be 875mph (1408kph), and that it would be achieved in 1980! However, the author did not have the fore-knowledge of the invention of the jet engine or the taming of rocket power, nor that World War Two was only a few years away. He also assumed that the Federation Internationale d'Automobile (FIA) rules covering such attempts would not be ignored and then overturned by US speedsters. Whether or not it was his design that was shown as an artist's impression with the article is not clear, but it was totally impractical and would have required impossible run distances to achieve any worthwhile speed.

The Ultimate Land Speed Record

Killen's 1937 idea of a future record breaker! (Varndell Collection)

Killen's predictions, despite his lack of fore-knowledge, were surprisingly accurate when Ken Norris' designs for the Campbell-Norris 8 (CN8) are considered. This rocket-powered vehicle, which was never built after Donald Campbell's demise, had a projected speed of 825mph (1327kph) in 1965! More is written about this project in a later chapter.

The accompanying graph shows how the land speed record progressed since becoming an average of two runs in opposite directions, alongside Killen's projection, which, had World War Two not happened, might have become reality (although it's doubtful that jet and rocket engines would have developed so rapidly without the war). However, Killen was obviously an interesting and far-sighted person.

Norris Brothers Ltd became involved with Donald Campbell through Lewis (Lew) Norris. Born in 1924, Lew completed his early education at Lewes Grammar School in Sussex, from where he joined Harland & Wolff shipbuilders as an apprentice, and studied to become a marine engineer. During World War Two he worked in Harland & Wolff's shipyards in the East End of London, manufacturing landing craft for the invasion of Europe. Postwar he went to the Far East to work for Burmah Oil, but had to leave in a hurry when the communists moved in. Incidentally, he once told me the story of a particular episode when he thought his end had come. Standing on a jetty waiting to be picked up, he heard a communist gunboat coming round the bend of a river. He flattened himself on the deck against a packing case and they, because the water level was some eight feet lower, fortunately did not see him!

Returning to England, Lew was asked by a relative to design some woodworking machinery for Kine Engineering of Horley, Surrey. Sir Malcolm Campbell had left his shareholding in the company to his son, Donald, who, at that time was looking to uprate his late father's boat, 'Bluebird K5,' by installing a more powerful piston engine and powertrain with a 'prop rider' configuration, to compete for the Oltranza Cup. When Donald Campbell heard that the Americans were building a boat to take the World Water Speed Record held by his late father, Sir Malcolm, he decided to uphold British prestige and go for it himself.

It was soon realised that a propeller-driven boat could not comfortably reach the very much higher speeds required, so Donald decided that the record should be attacked with a jet-propelled craft. Lew did the redesign for both the prop rider and the jet conversion of K5, neither of which were successful in their record-breaking attempts due to the outdated hull design.

Ken Norris, Lew's elder brother, was born in 1921 and, as with all of the six Norris brothers, was educated at Lewes Grammar School. He became an apprentice at the Armstrong Whitworth Aircraft company in Coventry, and completed his formal education at Coventry

The Land Speed Record (Records Made over 2 Runs)

Copyright Donald Stevens 2009

The land speed record since the two-way average was introduced. (Authors Collection)

Bluebird CN7

The Armstrong Whitworth 52 'flying wing.' (Ken Norris Collection)

In 1944 Ken took over the responsibility of running the mechanical test and research department at Armstrong Whitworth, and taught at Coventry Technical College. During this time he became determined to form an engineering company with his brothers. When he completed his aeronautical degree at Imperial College, London in 1951, his lecturer introduced him to Lieutenant Frank Hanning-Lee RN, and his very attractive wife, who had an outline design for a hydrofoil-supported world water speed contender, the 'White Hawk.' Ken worked on the structural aspects and aerodynamics of White Hawk, and Lew produced the manufacturing drawings. The craft failed in its record attempts on Lake Windermere and now seems to have disappeared. Ken told me that they were never paid for their work but were offered 'payment in kind' of a type that he did not wish to discuss!

Technical College. His work at Armstrong Whitworth, especially on its revolutionary 'flying wing' aircraft of 1948, earned him the Freedom of the City of Coventry. At the time of writing, this flying wing concept is being developed by Boeing as its future airliner!

The 'White Hawk' hydrofoil. (Geoff Hallawell)

The Norris Brothers at the press launch of Bluebird K7 Hydroplane. (Norris Brothers Archive)

Norris Brothers Ltd was formed in 1952, with Eric, Ken and Lew actively involved, and started operating in late 1953. The company had been formed from a most unusual family of six boys and two girls. Father was a gas engineer in charge of the Burgess Hill, Sussex, gas works. One of the brothers, Philip, became a fighter pilot in the Battle of Britain and was killed in action. Four of the others became engineers and one an accountant. Both Leslie, a civil engineer, and Eric, an accountant, also served in the forces during World War Two, Leslie being decorated for valour (he would never discuss his award of a Military Cross, but after his death I learned that it was for personally clearing a path through a minefield so that the tanks he commanded could pass through safely), and Eric serving in the North African and Italian campaigns. Walter, the eldest, followed his father into gas engineering. Kenneth (Ken) an aeronautical engineer and Lewis (Lew)

a marine engineer, with Eric as the accountant, formed Norris Brothers Ltd, with Walter and Les available for consultation.

Given Ken and Lew's experience, they were the obvious people for Donald Campbell to turn to when he decided to go for the world record, so Norris Brothers Ltd was appointed as the design organisation. Construction of the K7 hydroplane took place at Samlesbury Engineering in Preston, Lancashire, and the story of its achievements are well documented elsewhere in such books as *The Man Behind the Mask* by David Tremayne; *Leap into Legend* by Steve Holter; *The Bluebird Years* by Arthur Knowles, etc. A very detailed booklet, entitled *The Research & Development of Donald Campbell's Bluebird K7 Hydroplane*, recording all of the design modifications throughout its years of record breaking, has also been produced by Fred Blois.

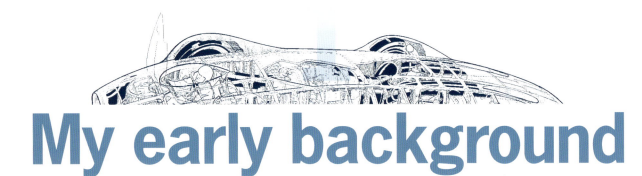

My early background

In March 1934, I arrived in the world in Stepney, London, the 15th child of an impecunious Cockney family. By that time only ten were surviving, the eldest with two children older than me, and the next married with a very expectant wife, so there were 'only' eight children plus two parents living in a three bedroom house with no bathroom and an outside WC! Five of the early children had died from the childhood illnesses prevalent early in the 20th century. Interestingly, much later in life, my mother told me that the doctors had told her that either she, at the age of 50, or I, would not survive my birth! Mother lived very actively to the ripe old age of 96, and I'm still very active at 75, which might be the reason for my healthy scepticism of most medical advice.

Schooling commenced at the age of three at Senrab Street School (now the Marion Richardson School) of which I remember very little other than an horrific 'Victorian' teacher, and having tricycles to ride at playtime. World War Two arrived, by which time my father was hospitalised with bowel cancer, and I together with my 'next up' brother and sister (ages five, ten and twelve, respectively) were evacuated to Haywards Heath in Sussex. There was some excitement at moving to the country, but on arrival about 50 of us were herded into a nearby garage where local volunteer families chose those that they would accommodate. Being a threesome we were not chosen, but were fortunate to be given a temporary home with six other evacuees and the 'Victorian' schoolmistress from London in, what seemed to us, a mansion.

This house, occupied by two wealthy spinster sisters whose family owned a chain of garages, had a large garden and a gate in the rear garden wall that led out to woodland forming part of the local recreation ground. The house also had a bell system which enabled the servant girl to be called to any room, a severe temptation for the older members of the group when left alone! Mother had stayed in London to be nearer my father and to look after the older boys who were doing fire-watching duties during the Blitz, prior to joining the armed forces. During the 'phoney war' I returned to London only to get caught in the early stages of the 'Blitz,' so was rapidly sent back to Haywards Heath. A few months later, I contracted what was known as 'German Measles' and suffered more than necessary because my brother convinced me that I was covered in Swastikas, but I did not have the sense to look in a mirror!

Several 'homes' were experienced before my mother moved to Haywards Heath, father having died and elder brothers now in the Army, Navy and Air Force. Temporary school accommodation and crowded classes did not prevent my teachers drumming sufficient sense into me to pass my 'Scholarship' examination, and go to grammar school in Hove. An undistinguished time there (apart from being caned for something I didn't do five minutes before my final English exam) somehow left me with a wish to become an engineer.

Brighton Technical College offered me a full-time place, but family financial circumstances required me to earn my keep. Fortunately, one of my older brothers, recently demobilised from the Royal Navy, was dating the daughter of the chairman of Allen West & Co Ltd, an electrical switchgear manufacturer located in Brighton, and, after interviewing me at his home, he arranged for my employment in the factory to learn manufacturing processes. Normally, I would have been expected to become an apprentice, but I did not want that length of tie in, or the very low wages. I was very fortunate to be able to decide myself when I had learned sufficient in each manufacturing department and request a move on.

To start work at 7.30am at the far end of Brighton meant that I had to leave home at 6am. This made long days, three days a week, as I was attending evening school on an Ordinary National Certificate course in mechanical engineering, arriving back home at 9pm. Of course, there were three nights of homework in addition to that.

One evening when at the Technical Drawing class, about 18 months after starting work, the lecturer asked me if I was interested in moving to a job as a draughtsman. He had been approached by two engineers who had set up a design company, called Special Machine Designs (Hove) Ltd, near my old school in Hove. At that time there

was a great deal of subcontract work from the aircraft industry due to 'Cold War' activity, and because a great many skilled people had been killed during the war. The company expanded, moved into offices in Brighton, and, at the age of 18, I was promoted to the position of jig and tool design draughtsman, eventually with four detail draughtsmen working for me.

Brighton was a far more convenient location for me, and reduced my travel time by about one third. Overall it was an exciting time in aeronautical engineering, and the company made an annual visit to the Farnborough Air Show. We were there in 1952 when John Derry's De Havilland DH110 broke up during a high speed run; a very sad experience.

My elder brother worked for the local Haywards Heath newspaper, and one weekend gave me a copy of an advertisement, which was to appear the following Wednesday, for a design draughtsman working in Haywards Heath. My application was delivered by hand to the offices of Norris Brothers Ltd before the advertisement appeared! As Lew Norris said in his 'Appreciation' earlier in the book, I joined Norris Brothers Ltd as its first employee, aged 19, in 1954, as a design draughtsman. Ken Norris told me, many years later, that I was chosen over other suitable applicants because of my upright posture when walking away from the offices after my interview! What would Human Resource specialists have to say about that these days?

Visit Veloce on the web – www.veloce.co.uk
Details of all books in print • Special offers • New book news • Gift vouchers • Forum

13

My other engineering experience

My first job at Norris Brothers was to assist Ken to project the film of the final crash run of Sir John Cobb's 'Crusader,' frame by frame, onto a drawing board. This was done, in a room with its windows darkened by 'blackout' curtains, so as to accurately measure the displacement of several datum points on the craft. This allowed Ken to work out the 'g' forces to which the craft was subjected before breaking up, so that K7 would have a much stronger structure. This gives the lie to the much written myth of these measurements being taken in the loft over Donald Campbell's garage. I was not there, but can only assume that Ken and Lew were re-running the footage there to explain to Donald what needed to be done. Besides, the walls of the loft were far too uneven for such accurate measurements to have been made.

The 'K7,' as the 'Bluebird' hydroplane was officially known, was designed in the company's offices in Haywards Heath in Sussex, not Burgess Hill as I have seen reported, with Ken and Lew leading a small team (initially consisting of just me!). The offices were then above the Bradley & Vaughn auction room in Perrymount Chambers, near the railway station. The team quickly expanded to include Ken Ritchie, a senior design draughtsman responsible for draughting the lines of the K7, and draughtsman Cliff Polley. We all worked up to 80 hours a week, and I earned the magnificent sum of £6 (per week!) for doing so.

Donald Campbell (DMC, as he was referred to at Norris Brothers, and will be throughout the rest of this book) showed his appreciation for this effort by giving me the photograph on the next page, taken when he broke the record in May 1959; the only record for which I was present.

Payment for the work on K7 barely covered salaries, so Norris Brothers had to secure other profitable projects. One of these was to become a recurring interest in my life. The company was engaged by a manufacturer of small electrical switches – Otehall Ltd, based in Burgess Hill – to design a high-gap microswitch, which it had been contracted to produce by Pye Ltd. Ken Norris produced the outline design, and I was despatched, part-time, to the Otehall factory to do the detail design. The project was successful and Otehall Ltd commenced production. Some 14 years later, after I had married and left Norris Brothers, my wife called my office in London to say that our Bendix washer/dryer had broken down. With two young children this was an emergency, so a repair man was called. On arrival home my wife told me that the malfunctioning part was not replaceable, other than possibly from a military spares shop. In fact, the service engineer had said it was something of a collector's item! Yes, it was 'my' microswitch. This obviously caused much hilarity at dinner parties – a 38 year old associated with the design of a collectors item! In 2002 my great

Photo of K7 presented to the author by Donald Campbell, with the inscription: 'Thank you for your support with this endeavour.'
(Author's Collection)

nephew, Nic Bowker, who had obtained a degree in aeronautical engineering, obtained work dismantling a factory that had closed down. Amazingly, it was Otehall Ltd, and he found two samples of the military version of the switch which he subsequently told me had become an 'industry standard.'

Another profitable project for Norris Brothers was the development of the production lines at the new Clarnico Ltd sweet factory in the East End of London. Existing production was based in a complex of rambling Victorian buildings and had to be transferred to a new

The Pye 401 microswitches.
(Author's Collection)

Bluebird CN7

four-story block designed by the chairman's architect son-in-law. We'd been given production quantities that we had to design for, and had much difficulty in providing them due to the fact that the building proved too short or too narrow, usually only by a matter of a few feet. Some new machine design, mainly in the packaging department, was undertaken. Our knowledge of air flow also enabled us to design new cooling tunnels for the chocolate lines, reducing their length considerably.

On-site work was done by myself and Cliff Polley, and proved to be an education in many ways. Work went on over the Christmas period and I was working in the company's engineering office on the last day before the holiday. The Chief Engineer took a phone call and asked me to investigate a problem in number three drying oven, a low temperature 10ft x 10ft box used to dry flour fondant moulds before filling. On arrival, I rolled open the door only to find two couples engaged in very amorous activity! Rapidly closing the door, I went to the number two oven only to find a similar situation. I then became aware of running feet and shouts of "There he is." A group of female production workers were evidently intent on putting me in the same situation! Being a VERY innocent 19 year old at the time, I ran for my life, managing to get to the office block, from which workers were banned, before being caught. The engineering office filled with howls of laughter when I entered looking very flustered.

That was not the end of the embarrassment, though. Clarnico's chief engineer told his counterpart in another local factory of our success with the cooling tunnel, and I was asked to visit it to see if we could make improvements. The company name, London Rubber Company Ltd, meant nothing to me, so imagine my embarrassment at the sight of women stripping condoms from their moulds and offering similar services to me!

Until 1958 all able-bodied males had to complete two years National Service in the military, and I had to begin mine in 1956. Normally, I would have had to start two years earlier, but had obtained deferment because I was working to qualify for my Higher National Certificate. Cliff Polley avoided National Service duty because of a problem with his hearing. For reasons best known to the 'powers that be,' I managed to get selected for pilot training, a somewhat rare occurrence for National Servicemen. During my time in the RAF, K7 was launched and broke the record four times. Ken Norris sent a telegram (an early form of e-mail – to younger readers) to me at Ternhill, my basic Percival Provost flying training station, when the record was first broken. I kept this, and, in 2006, when Mike Varndell was putting together the meeting of the Bluebird Supporters Club to celebrate the 50th anniversary

of DMC first breaking the World Water Speed Record, I sent him a copy. To my amazement, back came a copy of the letter, congratulating the team, which I'd written in reply to the telegram. Ken Norris had filed it with his records!

My flying career ended when one day I went out with a new instructor to practice low level flying. He was a very accomplished pilot, of similar age to me, but a very bumptious being, disliked by his regular students. After take off we flew coast-ward before descending to fly low over the sea. This being accomplished satisfactorily we headed back at low level. He gave me a course and height to fly, and I concentrated on keeping above trees and watching out for power lines. I remember thinking that we'd been carrying on for rather a long time when suddenly there was an airfield below me! I reacted by climbing as rapidly as possible, which woke him up from the sleep he'd been enjoying! Needless to say we had committed a major transgression, and were grounded pending an investigation. The fact that, as my instructor, he was in charge of the aircraft, did not prevent me being blamed, and I was not sufficiently astute to point out that he had been asleep. I was offered the opportunity to retrain as a navigator if I stayed in for five years, but that and other experiences of some senior officers, had made me disenchanted with service life, so I spent the last six months of my National Service as a Photographic Interpreter at Nuneham Park near Oxford. During this time Ken Norris told me that DMC had asked for a design for a new Land Speed Record car, so my decision was easy. The company had by then expanded and moved to larger offices above the Mid-Sussex Building Society, the Co-Operative grocery store, and a large private house in Burgess Hill, Sussex, with additional offices in Brighton and London. Another was opened in Reading, Berkshire two years later.

Initially, the project was not a full-time occupation, and I had to participate in other, more financially viable projects, one of which entailed being drafted into the Atomic Energy Research Establishment at Harwell, where a small group worked on designing emergency safety devices for unloading and cooling the early 'graphite reactors.' We were told that a 'Wigner Release' experiment was to be carried out at the Windscale (now Sellafield) generating station. We did not know then that the 'release' had already taken place, and that 'a Chernobyl' had nearly happened in the UK in 1958. It was not until early in the next century that officialdom admitted that there had been a problem, which was possibly the cause of higher levels of leukaemia and other illnesses in the area. During this time it was necessary for me to have access to the top of the BEPO reactor at Harwell, which was similar in design to the one at Windscale. I was issued with a radiation monitor tab which, fortunately, never showed an excessive dose. However, many years later I found that the current dosage limit was now one tenth of that at my time. So much for scientific certainty!

The Bluebird hydroplane K7 was still breaking records, but there was a problem in getting it to 'unstick,' i.e. break free from the water onto its planing surfaces. Although a step had been built into the underside of the hull to break up the water, the large flat area aft of the step created suction that held the craft down until about 50mph (80.4kph) was reached, slowing it and creating a large amount of spray. I remembered reading that a recent jet-powered aircraft had used air pressure bled from the fourth stage of the compressor of the engine to power some of the aircraft's auxiliaries. If we made a similar modification to the Metropolitan Vickers 'Beryl' and, via an on/off valve, blew it out through a series of orifices on the underside, it would break up the water. Ken thought this a good idea and I drew up a scheme and the company applied for a patent. (It is interesting to note that this idea was to be incorporated into the multi-purpose vehicle described in Chapter 9.)

About two weeks later, the telephonist called my office and asked if I would take a call from a "very rude and officious man." She put him through and the conversation went somewhat like this:

"Stevens speaking, how can I help?"
"I want to speak with a director"
"There are no directors here today; may I ask who you are?"
"Captain Farnsbarns-Snitchbag-Bigmouth" (or something like that – came the reply in a *very* haughty voice).
"What can we do for you?" I asked.
"I need to speak to a director about a patent that you have applied for."
"If it is the one concerning breaking up water adhesion, then that is my idea."
(Authors note: It was the *only* recent patent application)
"Right! You, the directors and anyone else concerned will be at your office next Thursday at 10.00 hours!"

"What on earth is this about?"
"You will be told next week, and this is a military order!" He then rang off.

Next morning I told the directors, and there was some consternation because that was a time of military preparedness due to the Cold War and we did not want to cause problems that might jeopardise the company.

At the appointed time, two Humber Super Snipe staff cars drew up and, from the front passenger seats, stepped two armed marines. They opened the rear doors and we were stunned to see two very senior Royal Air Force and Royal Navy officers (I have a memory that they were Air Vice Marshals and Rear Admirals) stepped out from each. One marine stayed on guard at the front entrance and the other at the door of the conference room where the meeting was held. We were told that we could not have a patent, could not use the idea, and, should any word of this get out, we would be put in jail immediately. No explanation was forthcoming, only that it was a matter of national security! When the hovercraft, designed by Christopher Cockerill, was announced about six months later we realised what the fuss had been about.

Ken, Lew and I looked at other variations of using the basic air supported principle, and came up with a sidewall design. This used the air support far more efficiently, having a 'skirt' only fore and aft. The sidewalls did not need to be deep in the water when running, so the craft could be used in shallow water, but not on land. A number were built as gunboats for use during the so called 'Malaysian Emergency.'

As a result of this design work, Norris Brothers obtained a number of military development projects. One of these, in which I was involved, was to design a landing vehicle that could propel itself through the water and climb a loose shingle bank, which neither the DUCKW nor the hovercraft could do. We solved this by supporting the craft on two hydraulically-driven, contra-rotating, 18-inch diameter tubes, which had 6-inch high Archimedean screw threads welded to them. The contra-rotation provided thrust in the water and pushed the pebbles together to provide grip to move up the bank. It worked and it was fun testing it, but I don't know if many were built.

Design of the Campbell-Norris 7 (CN7)

One evening in 1955, before a record attempt with the hydroplane K7, to divert DMC's mind, Ken raised his glass and said "Here's to the Land Speed Record." DMC's response was: "Yes, you'd better start thinking." Although no contract was issued, Ken began to think about a land speed record car and sketched ideas when they occurred to him, often on paper serviettes which he then filed away. It was a habit of Ken's to sketch on paper serviettes over lunch. I wish I had collected them, but such things were not thought of at the time.

When the possibility of an attempt on the Land Speed Record was firmed up, Ken began discussing his ideas with Lew and I. All previous record breakers had been powered by modified piston-driven

This and facing page: Ken Norris' early design sketches. (Author's Collecton)

aero-engines, but these were deemed to be of insufficient power/weight ratio for the speeds required to beat, by a significant margin, the existing record – set in August 1939 by John Cobb in the Railton Mobil Special on the salt flats at Utah, USA – of 394.20mph (634kph). Jet engines were still on the secret list in 1939, but by 1958 turbo-jet engines were available. A turbo-jet uses the principle of a

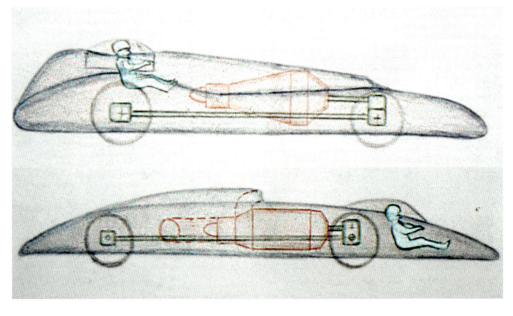

Design of the Campbell-Norris 7 (CN7)

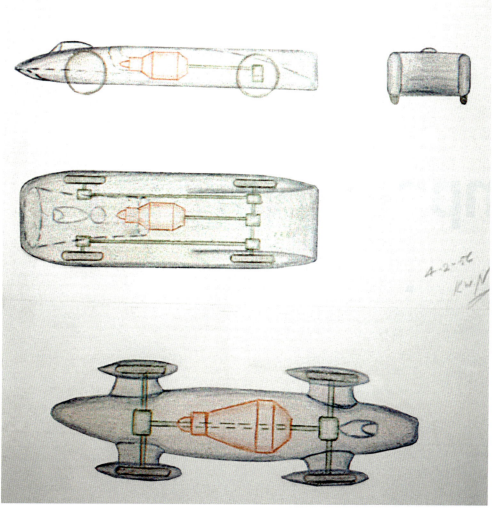

the design with very open minds.

In 1958, when we started to work on the project, the rules and regulations for all Formula and Record cars were set by the FIA. At that time it wasn't influenced by big business, as racing was less of a media circus than it is now. Advertising was present only on billboards around the circuit and in magazines, not on the racing cars themselves. The FIA's rules covering Land Speed Record cars were:

"It shall be a land vehicle propelled by its own means, running on at least four wheels, not aligned, which must always be in contact with the ground; the steering must be assured by at least two of the wheels, and the propulsion by at least two of the wheels."

DMC instructed us to work to those rules.

We were subsequently advised that we must also ensure that no residual thrust from the turbo-jet engine was utilised as propulsion. The only advantage that we could gain was to exhaust it in the best possible way to fill in the 'hole' in the air produced by the car at speed, which did give us some help as it smoothed out the airflow and therefore reduced drag. This ruling was later seen as laughable when the FIA gave in to American pressure to change the rules and allow pure thrust vehicles to challenge the record.

thrust jet for its power, but has discs of blades in the jet stream that, rather like a very high speed windmill, rotate a driveshaft that, in turn, powers a propeller through a speed reduction gearbox. With power/weight ratios of several times that of piston engines, one of these was a must for the new 'Bluebird.'

An often-asked question is: "How did Norris Brothers come to design such a vehicle with no experience of vehicle design." The answer is threefold. Firstly, Norris Brothers Ltd had designed the very successful Bluebird K7 hydroplane with very limited experience of hydroplane design, so DMC had faith in our abilities. Secondly, there were no obvious other possibilities with relevant experience; this will become apparent in the following chapters. Finally, we had no preconceived ideas as to what form the vehicle should take, so could approach

DMC, through his contacts in the Air Ministry, managed to obtain two Bristol-Siddeley 'Proteus' engines, which had been used to power Fairey 'Gannet' anti-submarine search and destroy aircraft. The engines had also powered the Bristol 'Britannia' airliner, nicknamed 'The Whispering Giant' because of the much lower noise produced by turbo-jets. I believe that, due to the modifications introduced by Norris Brothers Ltd,

Bluebird CN7

they were later used as power for emergency electricity generation packs.

Being a free-turbine, this engine had very suitable torque/speed characteristics, and wouldn't require a change-ratio gearbox in the drive system since the gas flow powering the turbine was effectively a 'fluid drive.' With that as the basis of the design, we drew up a specification from which the design team could begin working. This laid down the guidelines to be used in the development of the final design, as shown in the accompanying excerpts and drawings. It was clear that, to give maximum acceleration, four driven wheels would be required, and, as it had been decided that only four driven wheels would be used in order to keep the mass to be accelerated as low as possible, a drive to all wheels was necessary.

My copy of that document is number 12 of 12 produced with interleaved carbon paper, and is almost illegible, so it is reproduced here in retyped form.

(Author's Note:- The metric weights, speeds, etc have been added for this book).

Start of specification document

ANALYSIS OF PROJECT 18D

KW Norris
LH Norris
DL Stevens
10th March, 1958

Analysis of project:
1. Basic requirements
2. Model tests
3. Calculations
4. Design
5. Manufacture
6. Trials

1. BASIC REQUIREMENTS

a) Speed
Record average – 450mph (724kph)
Peak – 475mph (764kph)*

b) Course length
11 miles (17.70km) maximum on Salt Flats, Utah, USA

c) AUW
To be minimum possible.*
Maximum up to 9000 (4081kg) plus 1000 (455kg) equivalent weight of wheels.
Target for 7000 (3175kg) plus actual for wheels already designed.

d) Engine
Proteus 705 using maximum bhp and minimum jet thrust.

e) Transmission
Four-wheel-drive – solid unless proved impracticable i.e. no differential between pairs of wheels and no differential between wheels. Provision arranged for driving one wheel only for demonstration purposes.

f) Suspension
Fully independent. Stroke vertically – maximum +/- 2in (5.08cm) – wheels to remain parallel to normal plane during deflection.

g) Wheels
52in (1.32m) diameter over tyres. Hub arrangement to be agreed with Dunlops.

h) Tyres
Ref. Dunlops.

i) Brakes
Ref. Dunlops Transmission brakes to operate at and below 400mph (640kph) (ref. Dunlop letter 31.12. 57).
Air brakes – to operate at top speed.
Trans. brakes to hold 2 x full load torque.

j) Steering
Front wheels only. Max angular travel to suit circle of 150ft (38.10m) or +/- 5° if this gives a smaller radius. Not power assisted unless steering loads high or weight saving important.

k) CG
As low as possible and be such that tyres have minimum differential slip loads.

l) Thrust line
As low as possible.

m) Clearance
4in (9.6cm) minimum or 2in (5.08cm) clear with one tyre flat and suspension in normal position.

n) Fuel capacity
Sufficient for a run each way, plus 25 per cent extra.

o) Torque reaction
This to be balanced through the structure of the machine i.e. no differential torque load imparted to suspension.

subject to calculations.

p) Structure
This may consist of –
1. A basic space frame type chassis to take the main loads with a light quickly detachable body/fairing providing maximum accessibility. Ref. Fig.1.
or
2. An 'egg box' type body contoured, fabricated beam construction to take the main loads with fixed or removable shell pieces, depending on accessibility requirements, the compartments of the 'egg box' forming engine bay, plenum chamber, gearbox housing, cockpit, wheel housings, etc. Ref. Fig.2.

In both the above cases the suspension should, if possible, allow the car to tilt in order to meet the aerodynamic requirements (see later). The strength of the structure should be such that under vertical loading the SF (Safety Factor - ed) based on ultimate strength shall not be less than 4 and based on 0.1 per cent proof stress shall not be less than 3. This latter allows a factor of 1.5 for dynamic loading and a SF on this of 2. The engine torque should be balanced out through the structure and the stiffness of the structure should be such that the load distribution on the wheels is no more than 5 per cent different from static load.

q) Provision for one pilot
Semi-reclining.

r) Provision for air breathing

s) Provision for RT

t) Cockpit
To be sealed internally and externally to prevent access of salt.

u) Starting equipment
All to be external.

v) Wheel boxes
To be sealed from remainder of body as much as possible.

w) Wheel base
To be decided by CG and transmission requirements.

x) Track
To be decided by shaft angle, space consideration and overturning cases.

y) Fuel tank
To be positioned as close to CG as possible.

z) Aerodynamics
1) Air lift
To be as near zero as possible, throughout speed range but particularly in high speed range.
2) Air lift pitching moment
As above.
3) Air drag
To be minimum possible.

aa) Stability
i) Static
The air lift pitching moment plus the air drag/thrust moment should not exceed weight restoring moment at 1° positive incidence and up to a minimum speed of 500mph (804kph) The air lift pitching moment plus the transmission brake/drag inertia moment must be balanced by the suspension restoring moment at negative incidence corresponding to approx 50per cent deflection and up to a minimum speed of 400mph (579kph).
ii) Dynamic stability
The suspension must be such that pitching oscillations of the car are damped out in not more than one cycle, due allowance being made for the aerodynamic pitching moment characteristics, A study is to be made of Ref. 1 to see if any of the information therein is relevant.

Bluebird CN7

ab) Drawings

These should be done in car-line wherever possible and to a 10in grid space, reference plans being as indicated in Fig 3. A drawing register giving 'Drawing No,' 'Title,' 'Drawn by' and 'Date' must be kept.

ac) Calculations

These should be kept separate from design notes wherever reasonably possible. Pages should be numbered so that cross references may be made. An index giving 'Calculation No,' 'Title,' 'Compiled by,' and 'Date' must be made of all calculations.

ad) Graphs

These should be numbered, dated and initialled and have the formula or reference to the formula from which the graphs were derived clearly shown.

ae) Initiation of design work

To enable design work to proceed, it is suggested that with engine fitted horizontally between the wheels, the engine centre-line coinciding with the wheel centres, the body nose-tail line should be tilted 3in (7.62mm) down at the nose end, 3in up at the rear, approx, the rotation centre being midway between the wheels. Any extra adjustment of the suspension necessary to obtain the aerodynamic conditions required, if made down and up fore and aft respectively will then rotate the body about this centre Ref. Fig 3. In this manner the attitude and position of the body relative to the ground may be controlled.

af) Checking

All calculations and drawings must be checked and initialled, indication of checking on the separate items being evident.

2. MODEL TESTS – Aerodynamics

These are to include the following –

a) Model scale

1/8 FS (Full Size   cd).

b) Flow

To be made turbulent at a distance from the nose of the model corresponding to the full scale estimated position of breakaway, from laminar to turbulent flow.

c) Models

To be made in unit form, i.e. comprising of basic central model shape onto which nose, tail, cockpit and wheel fairings of varying shapes may be added, Plasticene being used to smooth in the lines. Intake to be incorporated with straight through hole to exhaust, a throttle arrangement being incorporated.

d) Tests

To be based on the assumption that the W/T at London University will be available. If so, the same false floor as used for the boat can be employed and tests run at a max speed of 170ft/sec (51.82m/sec). Hence scaling will be necessary to obtain full scale results for FS top speed in a similar manner to the K7 hydroplane result.

e) Tests

Are required to determine a body shape for minimum drag, an attitude for zero lift and pitching moment and the pressure shell diagram and suitability of intake.

f) Range of tests

Speed 150ft/sec (45.72m/sec) constant:

i) Pitch

Lift, drag and pitching moment to be measured over a range of pitch angle +5° to -2° max readings being taken at every degree interval. The normal being that indicated at 1 ae).

ii) Yaw

Side load, drag and yawing moment to be measured over a range of yaw angle 0° to 10° max readings being taken every degree up to 4° and then every 2°.

iii) Air brakes

Effect on drag and trim to be determined for cascade and other possible forms of brakes.

iv) Pressure Plots

Static pressure to be measured:

a) At intervals along body profile given by vertical centre plane.

b) At intervals along profile at max width.

c) At selected stations between (a) and (b) sufficient to enable pressure shell to be plotted. This to be carried out at incidence corresponding to zero lift and at +1° and -1° from this incidence.

d) Intake tests – Relative efficiency of pilot and under-surface intake.

g) Calculations

Are required to show:
 i) Position of turbulent flow wire and diameter of wire.
 ii) Weight and CG of models.
 iii) Strength of string and other apparatus.

h) Standard forms

These to be used for taking down and analysing results. Forms required may be determined from previous tests on K7 hydroplane, with additions for taking down pressure plots.

3. CALCULATIONS

These must cover:

a) Peak speed

Required for 450mph (724kph) average.

b) Optimum weight

c) Weight, CG and Inertia analyses

d) Gyroscopic effects

Engine and wheels.

e) Intake and exhaust duct calcs

To ensure that flow is smooth, capacity sufficient, and differential thermal expansion considered.

f) Suspension

Spring rate and damping.

g) Stability

Static and dynamic

h) Shaft wind-up

i) Impact on wheels and shafting of wheel hop

Ref. letter to Bristol Aero Engines, Mr Boardman. 8.3.57.

j) Performance

 i) Speed-distance and speed-time relationships during acceleration up to peak speed.
 ii) Speed-distance and speed-time relationships during braking.

k) Loading cases

Case A

Steady speed with vertical accelerations determined from unevenness of ground surface. If unevenness cannot be found however, it may be necessary to work back from a Safety Factor based on max weight limitation and determine the limiting operating surface conditions.

Case B

Acceleration.

Case C

Braking.

Case D

Turning.

Case E

Correcting course at high speed.

l) Stressing (including stiffness calculations)

 i) Main frame
 ii) Body
 iii) Transmission – Shafting, gearboxes, etc, (including whirling calculations)
 iv) Suspension
 v) Brakes – Air and transmission
 vi) Steering
 vii) Pilot's seat
 viii) Wheels
 ix) Canopy
 x) Mounting of equipment (fuel tank, etc)

m) Analysis of W/T results

To determine full scale lift, drag, pitching moment and pressure distribution up to maximum speed.

4. DESIGN

Work may be split up under the following major headings:

Ref. 18D 1 Engine

Proteus 705 with the following modifications:

a) Front end

Propeller reduction gearbox to be removed and new shaft incorporated from engine free turbine shaft to front transmission gearbox.

b) Rear end

New shaft to be fitted between engine free turbine shaft and rear transmission gearbox, passing through exhaust duct.

c) Governing

Three governing systems are envisaged. Ref. 'Proteus Prop Turbine Engine for Marine Applications' Section 3, 'Fuel Systems and Engine Controls.' As removal of the propeller reduction gear eliminates the auxiliary drive to the power turbine governor, a new drive for the power turbine over-speed governor will be required. Ref. BAE letter from Mr Emmerson 19.3.57, depending upon the basic front arrangement and/or accessibility.

d) Mounting

This may be similar for that of the Proteus 1250 Marine turbine or similar to the arrangement mentioned in BAE letter from Mr Emmerson 19.3.57, depending upon the basic front arrangement and/or accessibility.

e) Cooling

Jet pipe cooling may be arranged by allowing air to pass through aft plenum chamber bulkhead. Ref. notes 1B/3 meeting with BAE 25.4.56.

f) Insulation

Structure and skinning may be insulated from hot engine parts using 'Refrasil' insulation.

Ref. 18D 2 Transmission

A four-wheel-drive is proposed, a main shaft coming from each end of the engine to a spiral-bevel gearbox feeding each pair of wheels, there being no differential between wheels and pairs of wheels. Loading due to transmission wind up must be considered and reference should be made to (2).

Bearing information can be obtained from British Timken, who have already carried out certain load tests.

Couplings must be constant speed.

One wheel drive to be considered for demonstration runs.

Ref. 18D 3 Wheels and tyres

These are being supplied by the Dunlop Wheel and Brake Co Ltd, and the Dunlop Tyre Co, who are now conducting tests. The suggested type are 52in (1.32m) O/D by 7.8in (19.8cm) wide and the wheels may be as shown on Drawing W.S.1266.

Ref. 18D 4 Frame

This may be:

1. Of similar type to the hydroplane K7 with extensions or additions fore and aft to carry pilot, intake, intake duct and exhaust duct, etc. The main centre portion may be of square section tube and is to carry the engine, gearboxes, suspension and other main loads. The fore and aft additions or extensions to the main frame may also be of square tubing, but of lighter section. Ref. Fig 1.
or

2. An 'egg box' type of contoured, fabricated beam construction, the beams consisting of LA (Light Alloy - ed) webs with formed or attached flanges. The webs may have flanged lightening holes where they do not need to be airtight. It is suggested that a main beam is run longitudinally either side of the engine, and a main cross beam each end of the engine aft of the front wheels and forward of the rear wheels respectively. The central box so formed can then be made the plenum chamber, and the corner boxes the wheel housings. Fore and aft boxes with secondary beams added can be made to house gearboxes, pilot, etc. Webs and skinning may be used to form ducting if convenient. Ref. Fig 2.

Ref. 18D 5 Sub-structure and skinning

The envelope, which may be purely for streamlining, must be easily detachable where access is required for maintenance, wheel changes etc., and must be strong enough to carry air loads and its own inertia loads. The material, probably light alloy, must resist salt corrosion. A possible arrangement of body structure is to have a fixed initial intake section and a fixed exhaust section, possibly embodying the air-brakes, a fixed under tray and an easily removable central section for access to engine, gearboxes etc. Another possible arrangement is similar to the above, but with air-brakes embodied in the central section instead of the rear section, the object being to affect air flow at the maximum cross-section. Where structure or skinning is subject to heating due to proximity of exhaust, stone cladding may be considered. Provision to be made for jacking, craning, towing and securing to transporter.

Ref. 18D 6 Brakes (mechanical)

These to act on the transmission and must be capable of absorbing relatively large amounts of energy, but over a longer period than is required of aircraft brakes during landing. Also, in order to keep the car weight down the amount of weight carried in the form of 'heat sink' should be kept as low as possible. Hence some form of fluid 'sink' is contemplated, where the latent heat of the fluid is utilised.

Development is in the hands of the Dunlop Wheel and Brake Co. Both disc and drum brakes are under consideration. Ref. may be made to (3).

Design of the Campbell-Norris 7 (CN7)

Ref. 18D 7 Intake and exhaust system

a) Intake system

As the flow into the engine intake is relatively slow it is possible to use a plenum chamber. The air intake where the speed is high needs careful designing to obtain a good flow characteristic, and hence this, together with the intake duct, may be incorporated into a fixed body section. The remainder of the duct or chamber connecting the air intake with the engine intake may be fixed to the main frame or frame extensions and exposed when the central section of the body is removed.

Ducting should be as short and straight as possible.

b) Exhaust system

Here again, ducting to be as short and straight as possible. As the rear shaft must pass through the exhaust duct, the duct must split into a 'trouser.' Provision for shielding, such as Refrasil must be considered outside with stone cladding inside.

Ref. 18D 8 Steering

To be on front wheels only and, if possible, of normal type, i.e. not power assisted. The connection required on the steering wheel must be such that no movement of the hands relative to the steering wheel is required to bring the car back on course from a 1° deflection. The feel should be of the order of 3 to 4lb (1.4 to 1.8kg) for a correction imposing ½g sideways.

Ref. 18D 9 Cockpit appointments and canopy

This to comprise:
 a) Foot throttle.
 b) Foot brake and parking brake.
 c) Canopy handle with interior and exterior release.
 d) HP cock on port side.
 e) Air brake lever on port side aft of HP cock (motion lift – IN, lower – OUT).
 f) Air breathing apparatus.
 g) Radio control switches.
 h) Dashboard with:
  i) Rev counter (power turbine).
  ii) Jet pipe temperature.
  iii) Speed indicator (combined with rev counter).
  iv) Accelerometer/decelerometer (priority position).
  v) RPM indicator (compressor).
  vi) Engine fire warning light.
  vii) Air brakes 'OUT' light.
  viii) Oil pressure gauge.
  ix) Oil temperature gauge (gearboxes).
 i) Canopy – This to be bubble type with anti-glare bubble for head only incorporated in metal door hinged along leading edge.

Ref. 18D 10 Controls

1) Steering

18in dia (45.7cm) wheel coupled to mechanical linkage based on conventional type steering system, Ref. 18D 8 for steering ratio. Hydraulic linkage may be considered if mechanical is not adaptable.

2) Engine controls

Bloctube system may be used here.

3) Brakes

 a) Foot brake to be hydraulically operated on four wheels with mechanical connection (Bloctube) from handbrake.
 b) Air-brakes to be mechanically released and replaced whilst car is stationary, and must lock out when open.

Ref. 18D 11 Air brakes

To be positioned and shaped as found by wind tunnel tests. Possible forms are:
 (a) Cascade Ref. (4).
 (b) Hinged flat or curved plates as on Victor aircraft.
 (c) Retractable baffle plates designed to create max wake by placing at max cross-sectional area. If two or more brakes are used care must be taken to ensure that operation is simultaneous.

Ref. 18D 12 Fuel and lubrication systems

 a) Fuel tanks to be as close to CG as possible (1 tank each side may be used).
 b) Fuel backing pump required to give minimum of 2lb/in² (0.36kg/cm²) at the fuel pump suction. Ref. letter from Bristols 9.3.56.
 c) Lubrication. Engine lubrication to be kept separate from gearbox and other lubrication. Ref. meeting notes 2(d) 29.2.56, letter 9.3.56 from Bristols and drawing P.T.S.4741.

Ref. 18D 13 Radio and breathing equipment

Two-way radio with 'press to transmit' switch on steering column (similar to car horn switch or direction indicator switch). Air breathing equipment to be used as on hydroplane K7.

Ref. 18D 14 Instrumentation

This to be as stated under 18D 9 with provision also for wheel load indicators or G meters at various points (e.g. near wheels). A torque measuring device on halfshaft and motor may also be required. Provision for camera to photograph instruments must also be considered.

Ref. 18D 15 Miscellaneous

Consideration should be given to fire extinguisher system.

Ref. 18D 16 Starting equipment

It is suggested that starting should be from the outside electrical supply as for the hydroplane K7. A 120volt DC is required, the maximum starting current being 350amps.

Ref. 18D 17 Operating equipment

The following items will be required –
a) A trailer for transportation and possibly for 'turn around' at end of run.
b) Quick lift (hydraulic) jacks possibly four on a base frame trolley for wheel changes.
c) Starter battery trolley.
d) Engine davit.
e) Engine trolley.

Ref. 18D 18 Suspension

There seems to be no reason why this should not be based on conventional systems. The flat surface on which the car is to run and the short stroke therefore required makes the problem relatively simple. Almost any conventional system may be used and fitted into the space available after other more important items have been considered. Hard stops should be avoided at the limit of the stroke, the spring rate being arranged if possible to curve asymptotically to infinite instead. The actual rate and damping required must take account of the stability requirements.

The suspension should incorporate De Dion type mounting for gearboxes with swinging half-axles, consideration being given to the following possibilities:

a) Springing
i) Air springs Ref. (5) and (6).
ii) Torsion tubes.
iii) Rubber.

b) Damping
i) Friction.
ii) Hydraulic.
iii) Rubber.

c) Linkages
i) Wishbone.
ii) Sliding pillars.
iii) Trailing arms.

Note – Information may be obtained on air springs from the Dunlop Rubber Co. Mr NW Trevaskis – Director of Development, and on rubber suspension and springs from Moulton Company (member of Avon India Rubber Group) who have developed the 'Flexitor' suspension system as fitted to the Austin 'Gipsy.'

5. MANUFACTURE

One person at least of Norris Brothers Ltd, staff will be required to liaise during manufacture. A list of interested manufacturers and possible manufacturers of components is required, giving the name of the firm, the person to contact and the telephone number, together with the assistance offered or required.

6. TRIALS

One person at least of Norris Brothers Ltd, staff may be required to be present during trials to act in an advisory capacity and to keep a log of runs. A standard form, to be filled in during trials, for recording operating conditions, speed, rpm, settings, etc, will be required.

References
1) *Design implications of a general theory of automobile stability and control* Whitcomb and Milliken.
2) *Transmission wind-up in vehicles having several driven wheels* W Steede – Inst Mech Engineers paper.
3) *Recent advances in the design of aircraft tyres and brakes* Trevaskis – BAeS journal March 1958.
4) *Preliminary low speed wind-tunnel tests on flat plates and air brakes* N Fail, TB Owen and RCW Syre – NOS Cp, No 251.
5) *Development of GM air spring – Motorist* Jan 1958
Applying GM air spring – Motorist Feb 1958.
6) *Air suspension for road vehicles* JH Gainsbury, *Mechanical Engineering* journal Feb 1958.

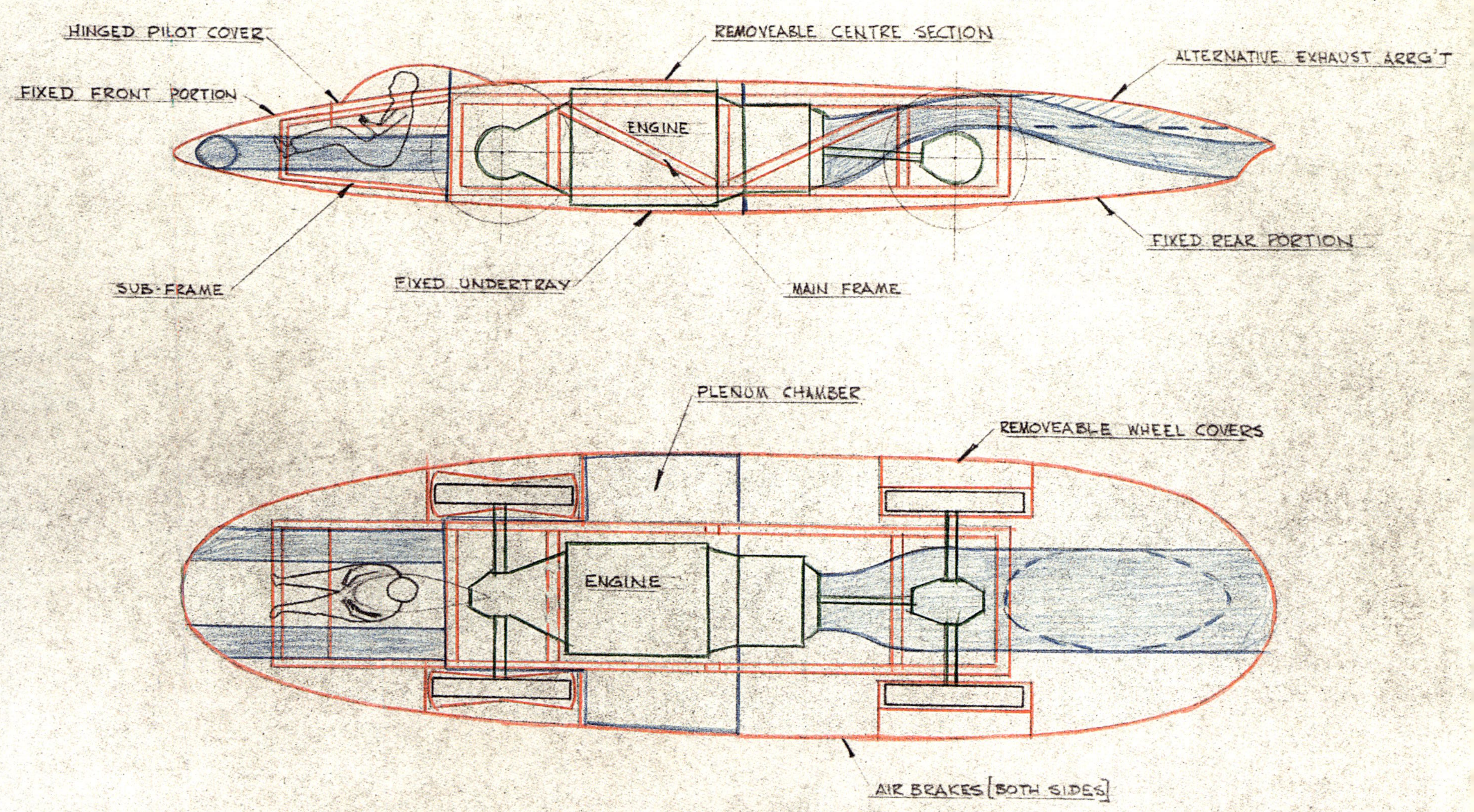

ALTERNATIVE EXHAUST ARR'G'T

FIXED REAR PORTION

REMOVEABLE CENTRE SECTION

MAIN FRAME

ENGINE

FIXED UNDERTRAY

HINGED PILOT COVER

FIXED FRONT PORTION

SUB-FRAME

REMOVEABLE WHEEL COVERS

PLENUM CHAMBER

ENGINE

AIR BRAKES (BOTH SIDES)

FIG. 1

Square tube chassis layout. (Bluebird Trust)

27

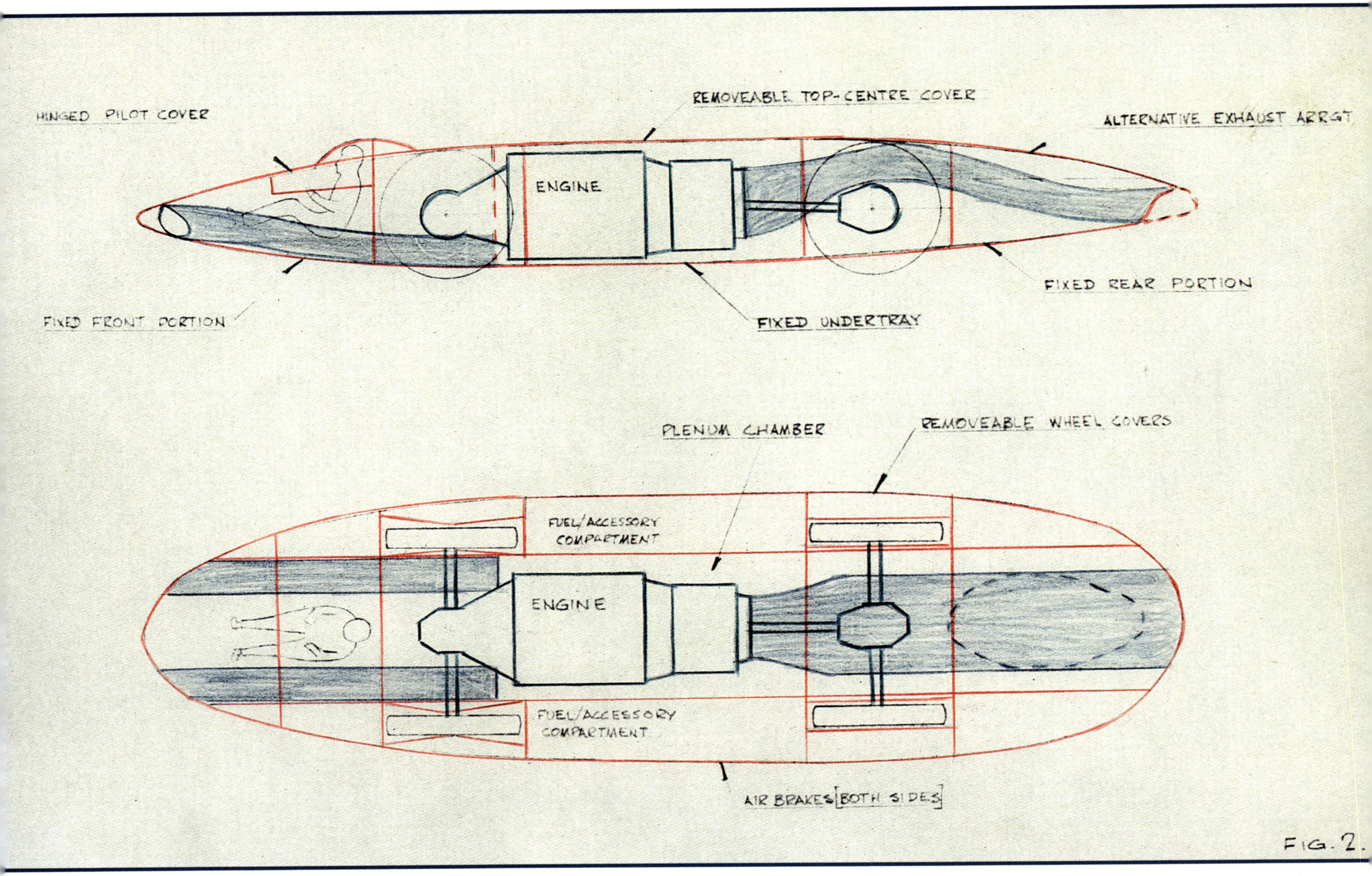

FIG. 2.

ALTERNATIVE EXHAUST ARRGT

FIXED REAR PORTION

REMOVEABLE TOP-CENTRE COVER

FIXED UNDERTRAY

ENGINE

HINGED PILOT COVER

FIXED FRONT PORTION

REMOVEABLE WHEEL COVERS

PLENUM CHAMBER

AIR BRAKES (BOTH SIDES)

FUEL/ACCESSORY COMPARTMENT

ENGINE

FUEL/ACCESSORY COMPARTMENT

Egg box layout. (Bluebird Trust)

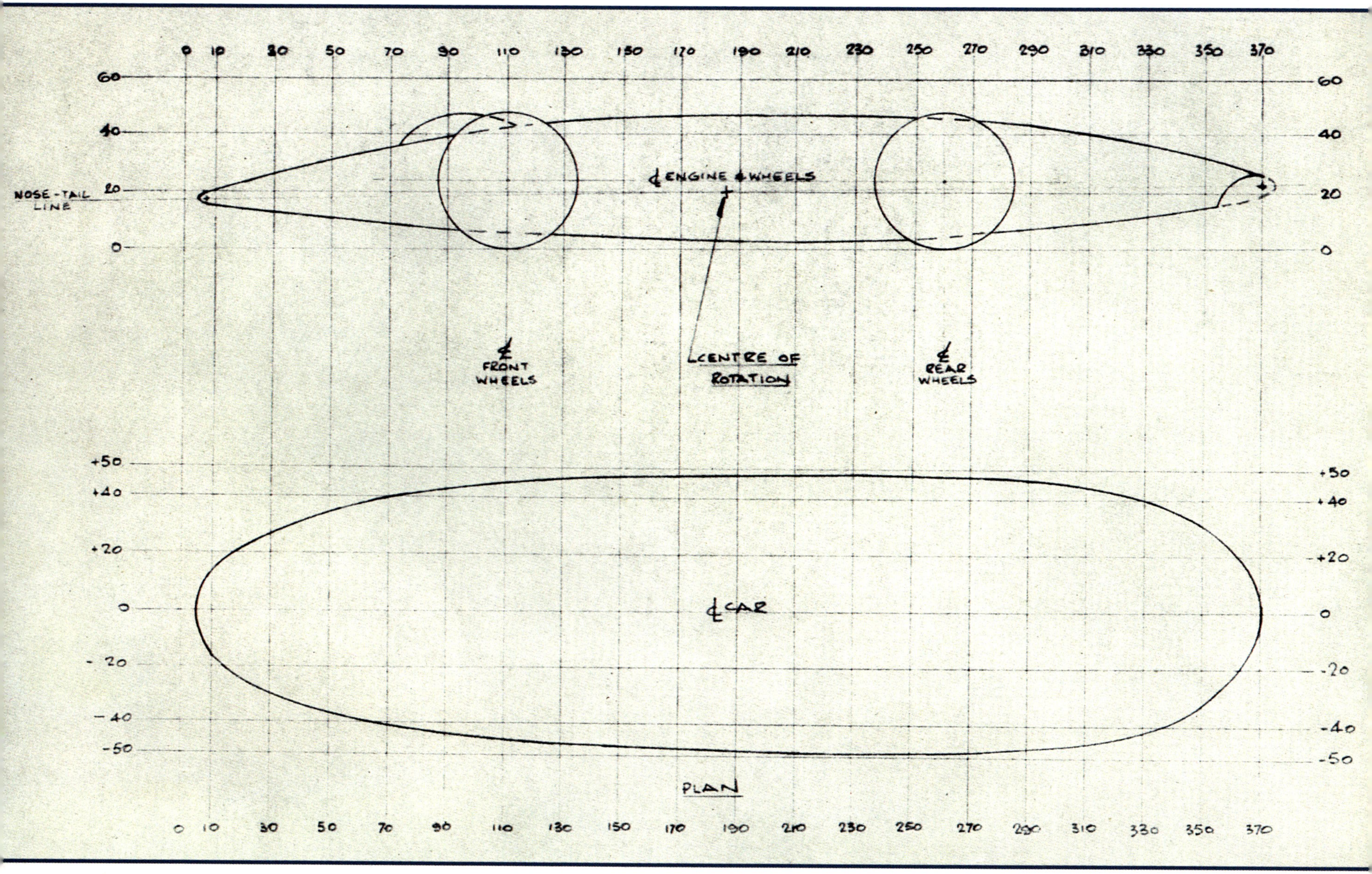

Datum line layout for part location. (Bluebird Trust)

60   40   20   0

370   350   330   310   290   270   250   230   210   190   170   150   130   110   90   70   50   30   10   0

₵ REAR WHEELS

₵ ENGINE ₵ WHEELS

₵ CENTRE OF ROTATION

₵ FRONT WHEELS

NOSE-TAIL LINE

+50   +40   +20   0   -20   -40   -50

₵ CAR

PLAN

29

Bluebird CN7

DMC involved the Dunlop Rubber Company to provide the wheels and tyres, and it specified that the overall diameter would be either 50in or 52in (1.27m or 1.32m), much larger than we had hoped, but with both benefits and drawbacks for design that became clear later; although with hindsight, the safety aspects were questionable. With the engine and wheels specified, we could now look to drawing up an envelope to contain them, and from that, design some wind-tunnel models to test suitable shapes.

Dunlop had made one further stipulation – that the aerodynamic shape should not provide downforce. This was a drawback from our point of view, as downforce would increase adhesion, and therefore the thrust through

the tyres; a valuable asset used by all high speed cars today.

Four ⅛ scale models were made, with their centre-lines, viewed from the side, going from horizontal, giving a cigar shape, to downward curved (cambered), so that the lower side of the car was flat. One of the horizontal centre-line models, and the maximum camber model, were flat top and bottom, with semi-circular sides. The other two had elliptical cross-sections. These were to enable calculations to be made after testing in the tunnel, to give the car as near as possible zero aerodynamic lift and pitching moment, so that fore and aft wheel loads remained essentially equal throughout the speed range, with minimum drag. The horizontal centre-line model was also hollowed out and the intake positioned 'as built' so that some idea of the effect of an intake could be measured. For the preliminary tests, this model had a solid nose cone inserted into the intake to equate it to the others.

Wind tunnel models outside Norris Brothers' offices. (Author's Collecton)

The team at the wind tunnel. From L to R: John Stollery, Leo Villa, GE Cook, Cliff Polley, Peter Church, Ken Norris, Dennis Burgess, 'Morry' Parfitt. (Author's Collecton)

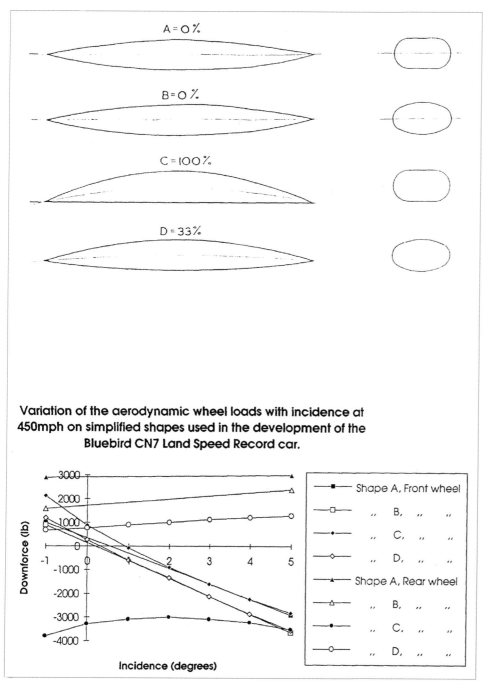

A = 0%

B = 0%

C = 100%

D = 33%

Variation of the aerodynamic wheel loads with incidence at 450mph on simplified shapes used in the development of the Bluebird CN7 Land Speed Record car.

Downforce (lb)

3000
2000
1000
0
-1000
-2000
-3000
-4000

-1   1   2   3   4   5

Incidence (degrees)

Shape A, Front wheel
     „   B,   „   „
     „   C,   „   „
     „   D,   „   „
Shape A, Rear wheel
     „   B,   „   „
     „   C,   „   „
     „   D,   „   „

Wind tunnel model shapes and wheel load graph for final shape. (Prof John Stollery)

professor of aeronautics at Cranfield University, editor of the *Journal of Aeronautics*, and a leading authority on vehicle aerodynamics.) We were permitted the use of this tunnel for a reduced fee, provided we allowed two graduates to work with us to gain experience of a 'real life' project. Tests were conducted at various heights above a fixed ground board (a moving ground was not available then). Although a rear fin would have provided aerodynamic stability in yaw (sideways swing) one was not thought necessary as tyre adhesion would be far more effective and there would be less drag, but one model was tested with twin fins developed from the two rear wheelarches. From the results of the wind tunnel work it was calculated that a 40 per cent camber would provide the required characteristics. At this stage a comparison was made with the Railton-Mobil Special, designed by Reid Railton and the then holder of the Land Speed Record. Despite CN7 having been designed on a 'clean sheet' basis, with no reference to the Railton or any other project having been made, the similarity between the two vehicles was uncanny, with many dimensions and the drag/weight ratio being almost identical; so we seemed to be on the right lines. It also shows what an advanced mind Reid Railton had; with virtually no aerodynamic information available to him he produced an ideal shape. A very detailed description of the project was given by Ken Norris to the Engineering Materials and Design Conference on 13th November 1961, and exists in bound form in Norris Brothers Ltd's Report No 61/18D/R.6.

As with the 'Bluebird' hydroplane K7, the 5ft x 4ft (1.52m x 1.21m) low speed wind tunnel at Imperial College, with a maximum air speed of 170ft/sec (51.82m/sec) was utilised under the direction of Dr John Stollery. (John later went on to specialise in vehicle aerodynamics, became

Bluebird CN7

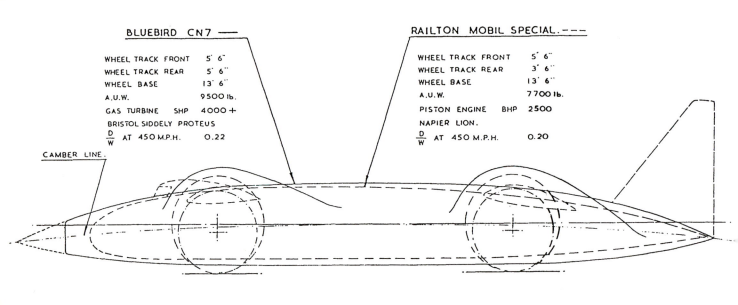

BLUEBIRD CN7 ———

WHEEL TRACK FRONT	5′ 6″
WHEEL TRACK REAR	5′ 6″
WHEEL BASE	13′ 6″
A.U.W.	9500 lb.
GAS TURBINE SHP	4000 +
BRISTOL SIDDELY PROTEUS	
$\frac{D}{W}$ AT 450 M.P.H.	0.22

RAILTON MOBIL SPECIAL. ― ― ―

WHEEL TRACK FRONT	5′ 6″
WHEEL TRACK REAR	3′ 6″
WHEEL BASE	13′ 6″
A.U.W.	7700 lb.
PISTON ENGINE BHP	2500
NAPIER LION.	
$\frac{D}{W}$ AT 450 M.P.H.	0.20

CAMBER LINE.

CN7 – Railton Comparison. (Prof John Stollery)

It is worth recording here a story related to construction of the models. One of the secretaries, Margaret Coates, approached me asking if it would be possible for her father to make the models for us. He was a pattern maker, a highly skilled craftsman making wooden shapes for moulding metal castings, and had some very well seasoned oak which he would use. The 'well seasoned' aspect was important because unseasoned wood in a wind tunnel would dry out and warp, ruining the tests. I visited him at his home and agreed that he could make them. When we had finished he asked if I would like to see his boat. Always polite, I said 'yes' expecting to be shown a small powerboat, and was taken through what appeared to be a door leading outside only to be confronted with a 15 foot (4.57m) high wall of plastic sheeting and battens! Passing through a flap I was staggered to see the hull of a 42 foot (12.8m) Bermudan rigged ketch towering above me. Although never having sailed such a craft, it had always been his dream to do so. Powered by twin Thorneycroft diesels, it was a truly magnificent construction with amazing attention paid to the craftsmanship. It was doubly interesting because his home was 15 miles (24.2km) from the sea, and there was only narrow access to the rear! It was eventually lifted out over the house by a giant crane!

Because the turbo-jet was designed to draw its air at low pressure from a plenum chamber – an airtight box from which it sucked air through its annular intake – and not as ram pressure through frontal intakes as with a pure jet, the idea of a box structure rather than a tubular space frame had obvious advantages. A space frame would need to be boxed in to provide a plenum chamber, adding weight. Schemes then started to be produced using the box structure approach. Such a construction would need large amounts of aluminium, so a supplier needed to be found. Fortunately, Norris Brothers Ltd had been doing some advanced railway carriage design for British Aluminium, so contacts were made and DMC convinced British Aluminium to supply all of the requirements. Technical discussions led to the idea of a 'sandwich' construction for the main beam, sub-main beams, plenum chamber covers, and gearbox chambers and covers. British Aluminium suggested that we met with a technically advanced adhesive manufacturer, CIBA (ARL) Ltd, of Duxford, Cambridgeshire, now largely known for its development of 'Araldite' (note the ARL, originally a British company, Aero Research Ltd was taken over by the Swiss company CIBA). Our original design was based on a 'sandwich' filling of thin corrugated aluminium sheet, but CIBA suggested that we use its aluminium foil honeycomb material called 'Aeroweb,' to fill the sandwich. This was readily accepted because it gave us weight saving of 0.53lb/ft² (1.56kg/m²) for the same panel strength. An approximate saving on the main frame of 125lb (56.75kg) overall, and well worth while. A similar construction, using aluminium foil honeycomb

Close up of 'sandwich' construction. (Hexell Corporation)

and carbon fibre panels, is used, 50 years on, for the 'survival shell' of modern Formula 1 cars.

In March 1958 the design team was enlarged to include Hugh Standing for engine modifications and power train; Fred Wooding for structure; Jerzy Orlowski for lines, bodywork and exhaust system; Alan Lucas for stress, stability and other major calculations, so that detailed work could commence. Gordon Dale-Smith, who had served his National Service as an instrument mechanic in the RAF was later to take charge of instrumentation.

Bluebird CN7's structure performed the dual role of supporting and housing the mechanical systems and human occupant, whilst forming the shell upon which a skin could be fixed. To provide the strength/weight ratio required and to keep corrosion to a minimum a BS NS5-1/2 hard material with zero per cent copper and

The design team. From L to R: Lew Norris, the author (seated), Ken Norris, Fred Wooding (seated), Jerzy Orlowski. Hugh Standing was away visiting Bristol-Siddeley when the photo was taken. (Norris Brothers Archive)

Bluebird CN7

3.5 per cent magnesium was specified. This was supplied by British Aluminium as its BA27 1/2 hard. Almost all of the structure was fabricated from 18SWG and 16SWG (1.2mm and 1.5mm) sheet, bonded and riveted together. Longitudinal and transverse webs provided an 'egg box' structure, each compartment housing particular items of machinery or equipment.

In order to minimise weight, single skin webs were pierced with flanged lightening holes, and, at skin intersections were flanged to suit the body profile. The main beams were 28ft (8.53m) long and 3ft (0.91m) high at their maximum, with auxiliary panels 13ft (3.96m) long. The picture of one of the main beams being assembled also shows the greater curvature of the topside of the car to give the required 'no downforce' from the aerodynamics. Note the solid aluminium inserts at points where major loads from engine, suspension, etc, were inserted; these were in BS NP5/6 (BA 28M).

All outer edges of beams and panels had a ¾in (1.9mm) flange for riveting, 'Araldite' bonding where possible, or quick release 'Dzus' fasteners for removable panels and covers. Where webs intersected, and across the honeycomb beam flanges, the flanges were joined with a capping strip prior to skinning, to distribute shear and compression loadings, thereby minimising skin loads. The 0.002in (0.005mm) 'Aeroweb' was bonded into the sandwich panels with 'Redux' adhesive for the main part, but in the region of the 9in (23mm) diameter exhaust pipes, 'Hidux,' which remains stable to nearly 300⁰C, was used.

Cooling the exhaust pipes, which resembled a pair of four-legged trousers, was also assisted by air induced to pass between them and the structure by the high velocity of the exhaust gases. Additionally, some parts of the pipes were lagged with a thin sheet of silica, batt sandwiched between thin sheets of stainless steel, and supplied by Darchem Engineering Ltd. Consideration was also given to coating the inside of the system with a sprayed-on stone to increase its resistance to wear, but this was not done as the weight penalty would be high and wear was not expected to be a major problem due to the short running time of the engine in this configuration.

Jerzy Orlowski's exhaust lines (shape) were a fine example of his skills. Remember, computers were not available back then, so all calculations to keep the cross-sectional area the same, whilst changing from an annulus to four equal tubes, had to be done manually, and the lines drawn by eye! The exhaust can be seen in the accompanying picture of the engine on the test bed.

The engine and gearboxes were mounted so that the extremely stiff structure, and not the suspension, took the engine torque reaction. By this means, wheel loadings on opposite sides would be almost equal, giving maximum traction. In its aircraft role, the 'Proteus' engine had a reduction gearbox fitted to the front to reduce the high jet engine revolutions (11,100rpm) to those suitable for a propeller (1000rpm). Bluebird didn't need this, of course, and so its removal reduced weight and enabled design modifications to take a power drive from the front and rear of the engine. This was something that Bristol-Siddeley was not prepared to undertake, but it did agree to advise us and vet the design changes. Later, it also agreed to produce the very complicated exhaust system that eventually evolved. Bristol-Siddeley was amazed at the

The 'Proteus' engine on its test bed. Note the special exhaust system for CN7. (BP Archive)

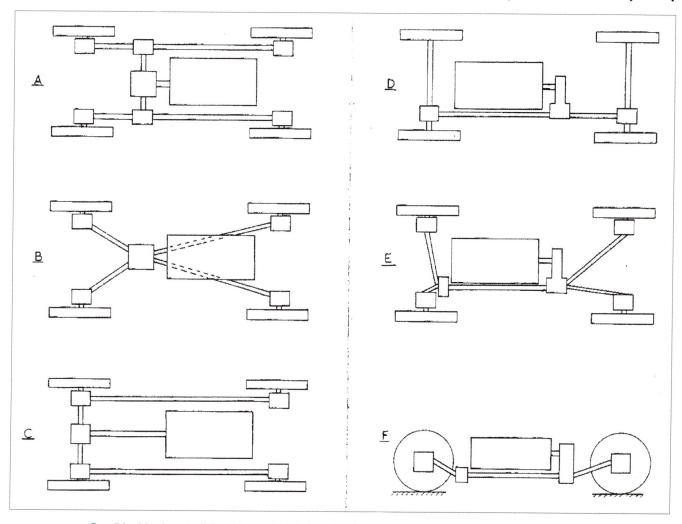

Possible drive layouts if the drive could only be taken from the front of the engine. (Author's Collection)

speed at which the engine re-design was completed by Hugh Standing, Lew Norris, and the team, estimating that it would have taken its team three times as long!

To meet weight distribution requirements, the engine needed to be placed centrally in the car, with the fore and aft drives going to speed reduction gearboxes between each pair of wheels. Dunlop had given us the choice of 50in or 52in (1.27m or 1.32m) diameter wheels, and it was decided that the 52in would best suit our purpose since the centre-lines of the engine and wheels would coincide, whilst allowing 4in (9.6cm) ground clearance under the lowest part of the body. This also simplified the design of the reduction boxes in that a spiral bevel rather than a hypoid gear could be used. In order to reduce shaft wind-up and tyre slip during braking, it was decided that a free-wheel device based on a Renold

sprag clutch should be fitted on the front drive between the engine and reduction box. The new, extended power turbine shaft, together with the couplings at front, rear and on the reduction boxes were made from forgings by Thos Firth & John Brown Ltd, and machined by Dowty Rotol, with the 'barrelling' of the coupling gear teeth being completed by WE Sykes Ltd.

The Dowty connection later resulted in Norris Brothers Ltd being asked to design a water-jet pump-driven power boat for Dowty Marine, which eventually became 'Jetstar.' Some further details appear on page 127.

The 3.6 to 1 reduction gears, housed in light alloy castings and fitted with a lockable differential unit, were detail designed from a basic design by Norris Brothers, and three units (one spare) were built by the Automobile Gear Division of the David Brown Company Ltd, then

Bluebird CN7

maker of Aston Martin cars. Each unit, transmitted over 2000 shaft horsepower and only weighed 380lb. Halfshafts manufactured by the English Steel Corporation then transmitted the drive via constant velocity joints of Birfield Ltd manufacture through further Birfield joints installed in the hubs. All of the ball and roller bearings used in the transmission were specially built by Ransome & Marles Ltd, even though all were standard catalogue items.

Shafts and couplings for engine and gearboxes were machined from forgings made by Hughes Johnson Stampings Ltd, in S106, EN100T and EN19U. Hughes Johnson made two additional samples of each, one of which was sectioned and etched to determine grain flow, and the other cut up to provide mechanical test pieces. Forgings were nitrided in oil at 900^0C, and tempered at 630^0C.

To complete the main mechanical parts we then required a company to supply the mechanical brakes and suspension, Dunlop having decided that it could not do so. The Girling Brake Company Ltd offered to undertake these elements, refining the basic designs supplied by Norris Brothers. In order to obtain maximum traction, it was evident that a fully independent system would be needed. Several different approaches were investigated, and the most suitable was found to be parallel wishbones with a tension leg consisting of a nitrogen filled 'air' spring pressurised to 750psi (51.7bar), with fluid damping. Maximum pressure on full working stroke rising to 3500psi (241.3bar) with a further 0.5in (1.27cm) remaining during which the spring rate rises rapidly. A working stroke of 3.5in (8.9cm) was allowed (total ground clearance of the body being 4in [9.6cm]), with rubber 'bump stops' incorporated on the outer diameter to provide further cushioning over the last inch (2.54cm). This leg weighed only 12lb (5.44kg) complete, and was tested to take a load of 2.5 tons (2542kg) on full bump.

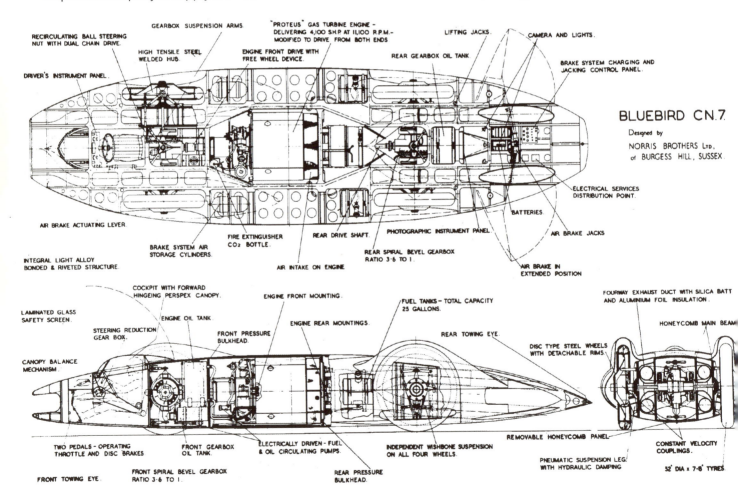

General arrangement drawing. (Bluebird Trust)

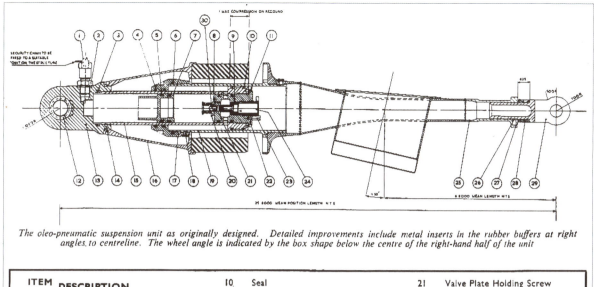

The oleo-pneumatic suspension unit as originally designed. Detailed improvements include metal inserts in the rubber buffers at right angles to centreline. The wheel angle is indicated by the box shape below the centre of the right-hand half of the unit

ITEM No.	DESCRIPTION				
1	Air Charging Valve	10	Seal	21	Valve Plate Holding Screw
2	Sealing Washer	11	Tab Washer	22	Valve Body
3	Seal	12	Spherical Bearing	23	Lock Screw
4	Seal	13	Cylinder Cover	24	Valve Plug
5	Seal	14	Grub Screw	25	Upper Body
6	Seal	15	Cylinder	26	Nylon Pad
7	Piston	16	Rebound Stop	27	Locking Screw
8	Valve Plate	17	Damper End Cover	28	Spacer
9	Seal	18	Locking Screw	29	Fork End
		19	Damper Cylinder	30	Valve Lifting Pin
		20	Valve Plate Spring		

Cutaway drawing of Girling suspension unit. (TRW Automotive)

These suspension legs have now had to be removed from the car in the National Motor Museum in Beaulieu, Hampshire, due to UK Health and Safety Regulations governing pressurised vessels. They would have to be pressure tested annually at considerable cost, so have been replaced by solid metal rods. At the speeds at which the car will now travel (mainly pushed by hand) they will be sufficiently effective.

The parallel wishbones required a sideways displacement of the halfshaft when the wheel deflected vertically. This was catered for under drive conditions by having a larger diameter halfshaft than was necessary for power loads, with long splines on the inboard end capable of sliding in the constant velocity joint. The suspension was made adjustable so that the angle of attack of the car could be changed by a small amount to equalise the dynamic loads between the front and rear

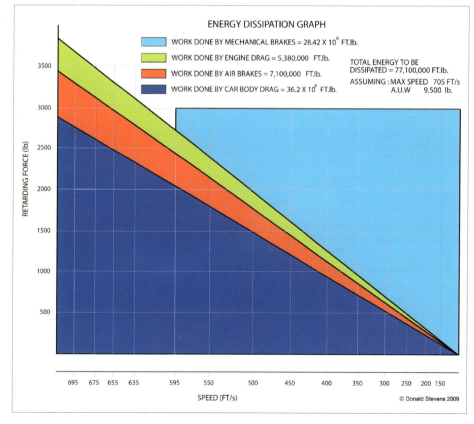

Energy dissipation graph. (Author's Collecton)

Bluebird CN7

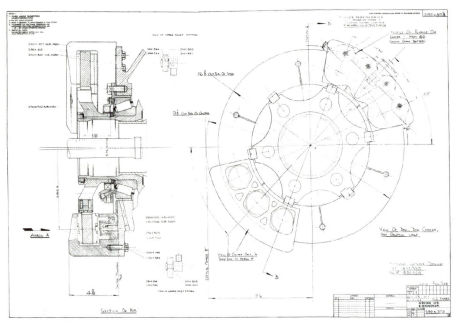

General arangement drawing of brakes.
(BP Archive)

wheels. Braking above 400mph (579kph) was to be aerodynamic, with mechanical brakes taking over below that speed. Both gave rise to problems. The most stable method of aerodynamic braking was to use hinged flaps on either side of the vehicle, but to prevent any yawing moment it was vital that they opened the same amount simultaneously. This was solved using a pneumatic/hydraulic operation with a mechanical feedback link. The main problem with the mechanical brakes was the high energy absorption required, 28.42 x 106ft/lb (3,853,184 Joules), or, in layman's terms, enough heat to boil 30 UK gallons (136 litres) of water from freezing point in 60 seconds! They were positioned inboard on either side of the gearbox to reduce unsprung weight. A number of sophisticated systems were investigated, including spraying the discs with liquid nitrogen, but a straightforward disc system was agreed as the most reliable.

The brakes were operated by compressed air from three bottles, two for main braking and a separate one for parking to prevent any pressure loss from the main system. The two main supplies were closed by valves until the brake pedal was depressed, whereupon a microswitch (one of the 'Pye' type that I'd worked on four years earlier) opened them, with increasing pressure being supplied with further movement of the pedal. In normal operation one bottle supplied the front brakes and the other the rear. If a problem occurred with the supply of air from one of the bottles, due to a broken supply pipe, for example, then a shuttle valve on each brake automatically allowed pressure from the other system to apply to all brakes. A stepped piston shuttle valve mounted on the upper calliper of each of the four brakes controlled normal and emergency supply. In the event of a supply failure in one of the systems that valve would be opened by the other supply without driver intervention. If both systems failed, the handbrake could be applied, but there would be no progressive action so it would only be used in the direst of emergencies; Girlings' engineers described this system as "akin to having belt, braces and safety pins!"

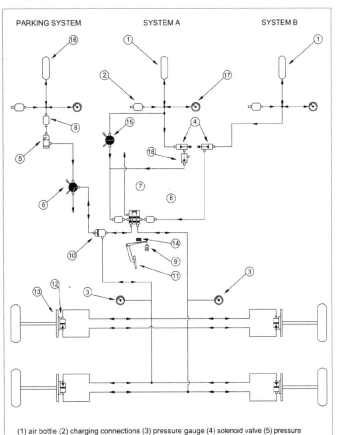

(1) air bottle (2) charging connections (3) pressure gauge (4) solenoid valve (5) pressure reducing valve (6) parking valve (7) brake control valve (8) line filter (9) spring box (10) shuttle valve (11) brake pedal (12) brake and system shuttle valve (13) brakes (14 micro-switch (15) manual two-way selector (16) parking air bottle (17) pressure gauge (18) non return valve

Copyright Donald Stevens 2009

Pneumatic control circuit for braking system. (Author's Collecton)

To minimise weight, the calliper blocks and pistons were made of magnesium alloy L125, and the and disc carrier of DTD 88C. Total weight of each brake was 53lb (24kg) with the 16.375in (42cm) diameter disc weighing 33.5lb (15kg). To eliminate judder when the discs attained high temperature, slots were cut into the inner diameter of the disc to allow for expansion. To ensure the fixing of the disc to the carrier, the six drive keys were frozen before being slotted into slots in the carrier which had been heated to 280ºF, and then held by two ⁵⁄₁₆in socket screws.

Ferrodo's team of chemists, metallurgists, mathematicians and physicists spent months developing the friction material for the disc brakes, and claimed that this produced "a pad which has just been subjected to more severe punishment on an inertia dynamometer in the Ferrodo Test House than any brake lining has ever been given in the world before." Three pairs of pads were used in each calliper, giving a total rubbing area of 78in² (50cm²).

Brake disk on test. (Author's Collecton)

Donald Campbell testing braking system on rig at Girling. (TRW Automotive)

Sponsors for the myriad of remaining parts then had to be found. With advice from the author, Peter Barker who was acting as DMC's manager, set about convincing appropriate companies to support the venture, with me joining in where detailed technical advice was necessary, or making the contact where only minor parts were required. Peter worked for a Fleet Street publishing group, but was seconded to take some of the load off DMC. A full list of suppliers and their contributions is given in Appendix 2.

Before detail design of the structure could be completed, the stress loadings that it would have to take had to be decided, and calculations made. With loadings

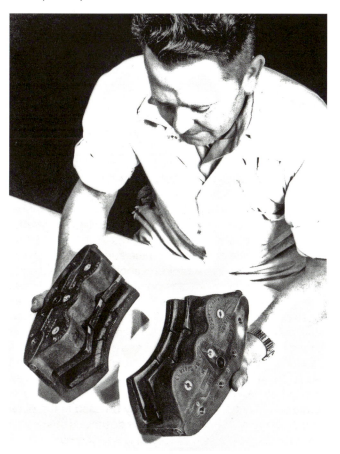

Brake blocks. (TRW Automotive)

Bluebird CN7

Girling's advertisements prepared for the 1960 attempt. (TRW Automotive)

due to aerodynamics, acceleration/deceleration, torques, etc, this was no problem, but the surface characteristics of the salt, such as flatness and adhesion, were needed. No data was available, and a visit to Bonneville was ruled out for budgetary reasons. Various engineers that had recently visited the flats were questioned. Their answers were respectively 'flat' and 'don't know,' and that from people designing class record breakers! Further questioning revealed that the 'flats' probably conformed to the curvature of the earth, and that hard 2in (5cm) high ridges of salt exuded through cracks every few feet!

Another subject on which we could find no guidance was the effect of caster and camber on steering characteristics. On questioning the chief designer of a marque that was currently breaking class records at Bonneville, we were told that they had no idea, and took a number of front axles out with them to see which worked best, an indication of the sorry state of British car design at the time!

Untreated salt surface at Bonneville. (BP Archive)

Design of the Campbell-Norris 7 (CN7)

Twelve major loading cases, corresponding to various manoeuvres, were devised for stressing the structure and major components. These covered acceleration and deceleration at zero and top speed, turning at constant speed, correcting course at high speed, and overturning at full lock. The main running case proposed loadings of 0g over bumps and 2g in hollows, but it was felt that this did not provide an adequate case for the suspension. Eventually, at the suggestion of Sir Reid Railton the designer of John Cobb's car, a loading case was devised which corresponded to dropping the car from a height of 6in (15cm). Over 30 structural tests were carried out to confirm the stressing calculations.

One final problem to be dealt with concerned the difficulties for the driver in looking out at the blazing whiteness of the salt and re-focusing on his instruments in the comparative darkness of the cockpit, which is clearly illustrated in the accompanying photograph. In addition to this, to reduce the possibility of wheelspin, some guidance was required to compare the rate of acceleration with speed. The idea being that, working from opposing zeros, the indicator needles should be centrally aligned for ideal opperation. This was solved

Contrast of light levels inside and outside of cockpit. (BP Archive)

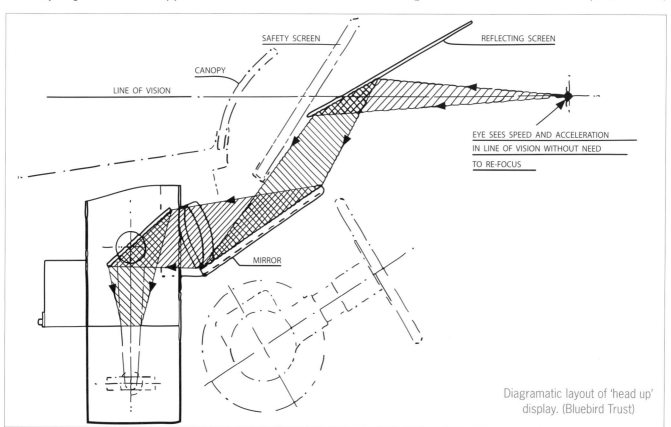

Diagramatic layout of 'head up' display. (Bluebird Trust)

41

Bluebird CN7

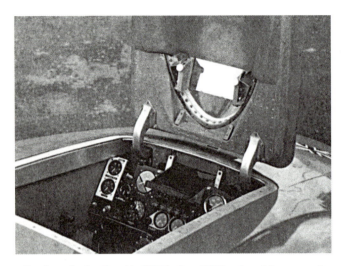

Head up display fitted in CN7 before DMC ordered its removal.
(Varndell Collecton)

by Smiths Instruments Ltd and Kelvin Hughes Ltd with, at that time, the very advanced head-up display being used in new fighter aircraft. The opposite diagram shows its basic layout.

Unfortunately, no-one thought to ask what colour the display would show up in, and when DMC tried it out for the first time at Goodwood, he instantly ordered its removal because the numerals and dial showed up in green; a colour he considered very unlucky! In addition to all of this, numerous other minor problems arose during detail design. Some were solved by Norris Brothers Ltd, and some by the component manufacturers.

At this stage it's probably appropriate to include some notes on the recording instrumentation that was installed to check 12 different measurements. The recording was done by a 'Hussenot' photographic recorder mounted in the compartment behind the rear gearbox, and connected by cable to each of the transducers mounted on the various components. This recorder had a motor driven removable cassette of film which had accurately-focussed spots of light that provided traces along its length. The spots were provided by tiny mirrors fed by a single lamp, screened from the film. The mirrors pivoted through the vertical plane in direct proportion to signals from the transducer to which they were connected via ratiometers or galvanometers, producing a variable line around a fixed centre-line on the film. The ratiometers compared the transducer voltage to its own source voltage and drove its mirror to a position corresponding to the difference. The galvanometer worked the mirror within a calibrated range based on variations in current. The recorder marked the film in half second intervals, and had a provision for

the driver to mark critical events via a push button on the steering wheel. Recordings were made of the steering arm position, each of the four suspension units, road speed (from which acceleration/deceleration could be measured using the half second time base), jet pipe temperature, burner pressure (a measure of engine performance), front and rear gearbox oil pressures, vertical acceleration, and ambient temperature.

A support vehicle required a 'darkroom' to process the film after each run. Gordon Dale-Smith was responsible for the design of this system, and for the installation of the telemetry equipment that was supplied by English Electric Ltd, being a very similar system to that installed on its 'Lightning' jet fighter.

The detail design was essentially complete by June 1959, a total of only 15 months, with 28,696 man hours and over 800 drawings; the most completely detailed design of a record car ever. During my research for this book I found an account, dated 4th May, of Norris Brothers' costs and receipts on CN7 up to time of shipment to the USA. It shows the following:

EXPENDITURE
Actual cost to Norris Brothers, including
   overheads, @13/6d per hour = £19,370.2.9.
Return   = £11,091.5.2.
Loss   = £8278.17.7.

(Note: These figures are in pre-decimalisation pounds, shillings and pence, 13/6d = approx. 64p)

This was a very considerable sum for a small company, and made Norris Brothers Ltd a major financial contributor to the project, as well as being the brains behind it.

British Petroleum became involved from the very early days because DMC was on a £5000/year retainer, with bonuses for record attempts with K7 and further bonuses for broken records, and a £5000 donation towards developing CN7. Its Sunbury Research Station spent many hours developing suitable lubricants and high temperature greases for the gearboxes, and its publicity machine went into action with still and movie photographic programmes. The gearbox problems revolved – no pun intended – around the high loadings of 290,000lb/in² (204.2kg/cm²) on the gear teeth at 11,000rpm, a speed that would spin off most lubricants, and the exceedingly high temperature developed by the mechanical brakes near to bearings and sliding splined shafts. BP also commissioned Norris Brothers to design specialist support vehicles, some details of which appear later.

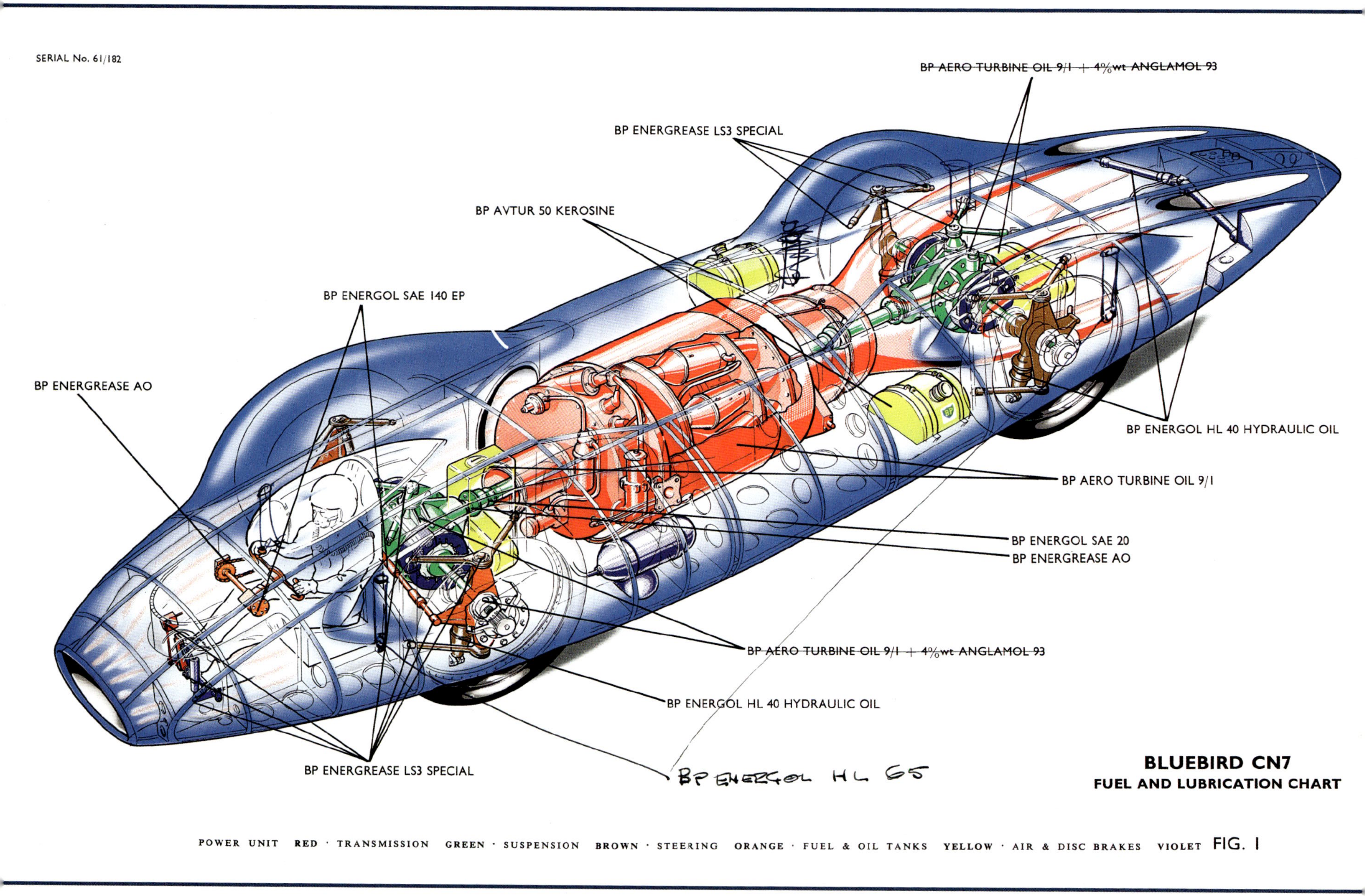
SERIAL No. 61/182
BP AERO TURBINE OIL 9/1 + 4%wt ANGLAMOL 93
BP ENERGREASE LS3 SPECIAL
BP AVTUR 50 KEROSINE
BP ENERGOL SAE 140 EP
BP ENERGREASE AO
BP ENERGOL HL 40 HYDRAULIC OIL
BP AERO TURBINE OIL 9/1
BP ENERGOL SAE 20
BP ENERGREASE AO
BP AERO TURBINE OIL 9/1 + 4%wt ANGLAMOL 93
BP ENERGOL HL 40 HYDRAULIC OIL
BP ENERGREASE LS3 SPECIAL
BP ENERGOL HL 65
BLUEBIRD CN7
FUEL AND LUBRICATION CHART
POWER UNIT RED · TRANSMISSION GREEN · SUSPENSION BROWN · STEERING ORANGE · FUEL & OIL TANKS YELLOW · AIR & DISC BRAKES VIOLET
FIG. 1

A never-used BP promotional lubrication chart which has the author's 1960 suggested addition of the jacking system inked in. (BP Archive)

Construction

In 1927 AF Rivers-Fletcher, the 15-year-old son of a well known Brooklands racing driver, rode in Malcolm Campbell's car as his 'racing mechanic' at Brooklands. He was the only person available that was small enough to fit into the space, and became a friend of the family. In the 1950s he was Public Relations Officer to the Owen Organisation, working mainly on the BRM. DMC approached him to see if the company might help with some parts and some funds. On December 1st 1958, Rivers-Fletcher sent a memo to Sir Alfred Owen, a very patriotic person and Chairman and main shareholder of The Owen Organisation, the companies of which produced parts for the automotive industry. The memo suggested that the company might "... supply all the nuts and bolts and fastenings ... and perhaps undertake some machining or supply ... other special bits and pieces." Sir Alfred's response was: "Our commitment on the BRM precludes us from making anything but a nominal contribution."

This and facing page: Rubery Owen Memo. Note Sir Alfred's agreement to spend £1000! (Rubery Owen Archive)

5/1

Rubery, Owen & Co. Ltd.

FROM		TO	
	P. SPEAR.		MR. A. G. B. OWEN.
THIS REF.	PS/PH.	YOUR REF.	DATE 26th January, 1959.

£1000 towards cost

Donald Campbell.

As arranged I visited Donald Campbell on Monday, 19th January to formulate a proposition on what components we might make for his car. I discussed it from various aspects and the following are graded propositions.

1. Track Rods. This is a tube with a steel ball at each end and approximately 8" long. It is a straightforward machining, grinding and heat treatment job. A small quantity only are required, and I would estimate the work to be of the order of £100.

2. Rear Drive Shaft. This is a tube about 20" long with a spur guard at each end. It is in effect a quill shaft from which power comes via gearing to the axles. From the heat treatment and machining angles it is fairly straightforward, but the gear teeth have a barrel section which complicates things. It is more a job for E.N.V. and I offered an introduction to Brian Wilson. I would estimate the cost at three or four hundred pounds.

3. Exhaust Ducting. This is panel beating and welding with suitable gas turbine alloy in 20 SWG sheet form. It is approximately 3ft. long, a single tube of about 2ft. diameter at one end where it clips on to the engine and branches into 4 tubes 9½" diameter on to which are fastened the 4 exhaust pipes. The work is fairly accurate and probably 2 at least would be needed. We would have to give some help in selection of material but this is not difficult. It should be a job suitable for Motor Panels. I would estimate the cost at about £1,000.

4. Air Brake Actuating Equipment. At the back of the car are two panels which open up by compressed CO_2 to act as brakes. They know the pick up points but want the hydraulic system designing and jacks, valves, etc. supplying. This is very similar in principle to air brake equipment as used on aircraft and it should be a fairly straightforward job for Electro-Hydraulics. I have little idea of here but I would guess £2,000.

Rubery, Owen & Co. Ltd.

P. SPEAR.	TO	MR. A. G. B. OWEN.
THIS REF. YOUR REF.	DATE	26th January, 1959.

— 2 —

5.   Complete Bodywork. They have not yet placed the complete body for the car. In the main it follows aircraft practice rather than automobile. It is a big job and is probably worth about £10,000. Their own estimate is £8,000. Apparently B.M.C. are interested in doing the bodywork. From a publicity viewpoint it would of course be a very attractive item, although personally I think it is a lot of money in a venture of this nature.

I left it with Donald Campbell that I would put up to you the graded proposition leaving you to make a choice.

Additional notes on the discussions are appended. You will see that there is as yet no opportunity on Nuts, Bolts, etc.

Director of Research.

Copied to Mr. A. F. Rivers Fletcher.

By the 26th January 1959, Peter Spear, Rubery Owen's Director of Research, after meeting with DMC, put forward a 'graded proposal' that suggested possible involvement in five different areas, ranging from supplying the track rods (estimate £100) to constructing the bodywork (estimate £10,000), and finished up by saying: "You will see there is as yet no opportunity on nuts, bolts, etc."

There is no record of how Sir Alfred was persuaded to change his mind to such a degree, but he soon agreed to build the car at Motor Panels (Coventry) Ltd, whose everyday business was to build specialist cabs for trucks. This was in addition to its subsidiary Electro-Hydraulics, which built landing gear for aircraft, supplying air brake actuators and controls, plus the car jacking system, and other group companies providing specialist machining. Without Rubery Owen's enormous contribution, it would have been a much more difficult task to get the car built, and, of course, it built the replacement one after the Bonneville crash.

On 19th August 1959, at a meeting between Ken Norris, the author, DMC, Leo Villa and Peter Spear (Rubery Owen), and Jim Phillips and Maurice Britton of Motor Panels, the programme of construction was agreed. Motor Panels laid down a special concrete base, topped with two steel I-beams, so that the main frame could be accurately assembled. It was equipped with mounting spigots that would hold the frame at its 'running height' above the ground, and was completed by December 1959. I sent 58 drawings of the main structure to Peter Spear on 19th September so that construction could start. The panels for the main and auxiliary beams were formed during this time, and were sent to CIBA at Duxford for bonding into composite panels with CIBA's 'Aeroweb' honeycomb on 5th November. By early January 1960 the main and auxiliary beams had been returned and could be assembled ready for the rest of the frame to be attached. The main beams were so well built that the maximum deviation over their entire 26ft (7.92m) length was only $\frac{1}{16}$in (0.041cm). With the main beams in position, the auxiliary beams could be attached and the sub panels beaten to shape and fixed. The accompanying photographs clearly show the sandwich construction of the beams and the method of reducing weight with flanged lightening holes in the sub panels. This phase was very critical in that every panel had to be made very accurately so that when the skin was finally placed on it there would be no bumps or waviness to disturb the airflow. For each panel, a very accurate wooden former was made to ensure no deviations in the profile of the car which might cause greater aerodynamic drag. This took until mid-March, when the mechanical equipment began to be installed and the outside skin put in place. Some very difficult panel beating was involved with the large wheelarches and bifurcated air intake ducts.

The main beams being laid out for glueing, showing solid inserts at main stress points. (Hexcell Corporation)

Bluebird CN7

Left: The assembled main and auxilliary beams. (Hexell Corporation)

Opposite, top left: A rear auxilliary beam with its cut-out for the exhaust system. (Rubery Owen Archive)

Below: Panel capping strips being marked out and assembled. (Rubery Owen Archive)

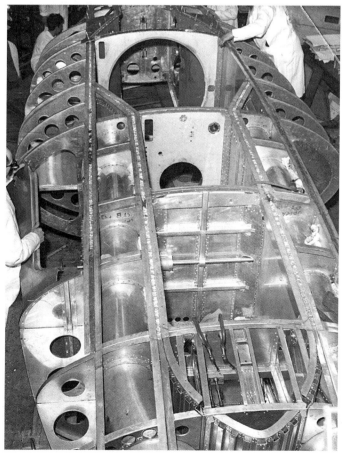

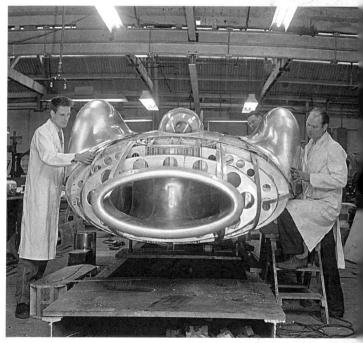

Left: View of structure looking aft from cockpit. (Rubery Owen Archive)

Top right: Assembling the top skin. (Rubery Owen Archive)

Above: Fitting front wheelarches. (Rubery Owen Archive)

Bluebird CN7

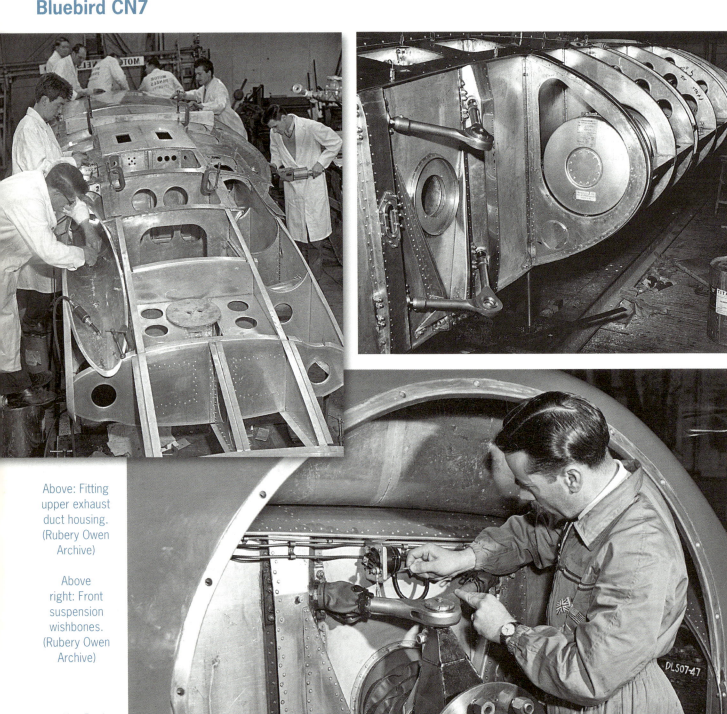

Above: Fitting upper exhaust duct housing. (Rubery Owen Archive)

Above right: Front suspension wishbones. (Rubery Owen Archive)

Ken Reaks installing suspension movement transducers. (Rubery Owen Archive)

Rear transmission box viewed from engine compartment. (Rubery Owen Archive)

Leo Villa, DMC's chief mechanic, led the team in charge of the mechanical assembly. This team included Maurice 'Morry' Parfit, Brian Coppock and Ken Ritchie, who had been enticed away from Norris Brothers, from the Campbell team, plus Cliff Polley from Norris Brothers, supplemented by specialist engineers from major suppliers. Ray Govier from Bristol-Siddeley, Tom Lawson from Lucas, Ron Willis from Girling, Carl Noble from Electro-Hydraulics, Ken Reakes from Smiths Instruments, and others from Dunlop and various suppliers when required. During June the workshop was often in use over 24-hour periods to prevent one part of the assembly process from interfering with another.

DMC and I would periodically make tours of the large- and medium-sized companies, but the smaller ones were left to me. When with DMC, we travelled in his Bentley Continental, and almost always were pressed for time. My car at the time was a very mundane 1948 Standard 8, so imagine my panic when one day, running late as usual, DMC pulled to the side of the road and insisted that I take over driving as his back was too painful to continue. Standard 8 top speed 60mph (96.5kph) with a following wind; Bentley top speed 120mph (193kph) and at least twice the size, and we were in a hurry! He made no allowances for my lack of experience driving large or fast cars, saying: "Well, if you can fly a jet, no reason why you can't drive this!" Although traffic volumes were very much lower, roads were still congested, especially in the Midlands, so it was a somewhat hair-raising drive. Later, when I was liaising with suppliers, I was given the use of either an Austin Healey 'Sprite' or a Triumph 'Herald' from DMC's 'stable.' Neither of these was particularly sporty in their basic form, but Leo transformed them into 'interesting' cars to drive. It was great fun leaving MGs behind from standing starts, but they usually caught up with the 'Herald' on twisting roads.

DMC found the Midlands a rather depressing place and after a few days there would often say: "I've had enough of this, let's go back to town." At that time the only motorway going north from London was the first stage of the M1 between Watford and Crick. A 100+mph

Meanwhile, parts were being produced by large and small companies all over the country, from Yorkshire to Surrey. Even 'standard' parts were often specially manufactured! Dunlop needed to build a brand new test facility to test the tyres and wheels because its existing one could not cope with the speeds or size required. Dunlop was gracious enough to admit that the facility would be needed for new aircraft tyres anyway! The booklet issued by Dunlop describing the new installation is reproduced in Appendix 4, and I understand that it safely tested CN7's tyres up to 650mph (965kph)! All these parts came together during March, April and May, with much adjusting of schedules due to delays in supply. However, the team, which now included specialist fitters from the major suppliers, worked together very well, and made allowances for each other's problems.

The engine arrived on May 11th, a seminal day in my relationship with Leo Villa, which is explained later, but it would take until July for the several coats of paint to be applied and smoothed to aircraft standard. Maurice Britten, works manager at Motor Panels, did an exceedingly good job of organising the body assembly, and the panel beating team under Tom Scrimshire (Jim and Ivor Sherrard, Bill Bentley, Ron Chattaway, Brian Kenney and Brian Lee) made a fantastic job of the panel beating.

Bluebird CN7

The author explaining the transmission box design to Donald Campbell and Leo Villa. (Press Association)

(161+kph) drive down the M1 (it was unrestricted then, and Aston Martin, based in Newport Pagnel, found it very convenient for speed testing its cars!), book into a 4-star hotel, dinner at Rules in Maiden Lane, and then on to the Embassy Club! On the first visit to Rules we arrived outside only to find a large 'No Parking' sandwich board in the only available space. DMC said: "Jump out and move that." I started to do so, and, as I picked up the board, a large shadow fell over me and a deep voice said: "May I help you sir?" It was the top-hatted doorman, and he did it for me. Influence counts! For a very innocent young engineer it was a very 'illuminating' time, to say the least!

After one such visit on our way back south, we returned to DMC's home, Roundwood, for me to collect my car, and DMC insisted that I went in to meet his new wife, Tonia. He went to his office leaving me to chat with her. Imagine my embarrassment when Tonia asked: "Did you enjoy yourself last night?" I was obviously flustered, and she said: "Oh don't worry, I know what he gets up to when he's away, but he always comes back

to me refreshed!" A very open-minded and attractive lady!

There was obviously a great deal of press interest in the project, but it was agreed that no press should be allowed any information until the official release. However, I decided that, for the sake of accuracy, it would be safe to allow Leslie Cresswell, the cutaway drawing artist for *The Motor* magazine to visit Motor Panels to draw the insides of the car before it was skinned. He agreed in writing to keep his drawings and knowledge to himself until the agreed date, and spent three days tucked into a corner of Motor Panels' workshop before deciding he had sufficient data to finish the task at home. Two days after he left, I was called to Jim Phillip's (Motor Panels' managing director) office, and received a massive blasting because I had allowed 'the press' in. The fact that it enabled an accurate drawing of the car to be done did not occur, or matter, to him. Leslie later sent me the accompanying 'pull' of his drawing, autographed by him and with the words: "It could not have been done without your help."

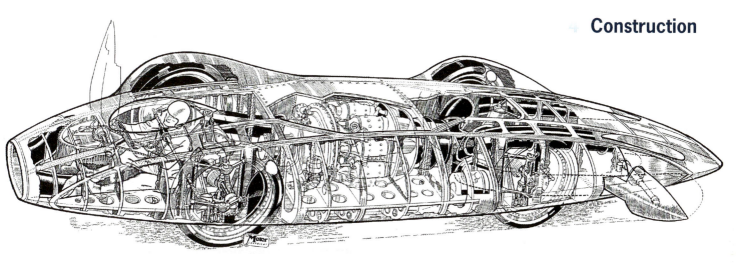

Leslie Cresswell's cutaway drawing with its dedication to the author: 'It could not have been done without your help.' (*Autocar* Archive)

I remember thinking at the time that Jim Phillips was too typical of senior management in British industry. He was overly self-important, had his own dining room with a permanent chef, to which he considered it an honour for others to be invited. I further 'blotted my copy book' when, on a visit from DMC and Ken Norris, I was invited to lunch with them. The main course arrived in a large lidded tureen which Jim ceremoniously opened with the words: "My favourite dish." When the odour reached my nostrils, I felt immediately sick! DMC asked the name of the dish. "Jugged Hare, my favourite dish," was the proud response. There was no way that I could stomach it, so I said that I would be happy to have just vegetables. Jim almost exploded, and insisted on calling the chef to make an omelette for me. On the drive back down, Ken was feeling very 'queasy' and DMC said that he felt unwell and admired me for my bravery!

The opposite end of British senior management was exemplified by John Sully, who had the title of General Manager at English Electric Ltd, Stafford – his actual function was Managing Director of its generator turbine manufacturing plant that employed over 3000 people. John was a very enlightened leader and offered to produce any miscellaneous turned parts that we needed. These were made by apprentices in order to give them a greater interest in their work. Another example of his approach was to obtain drawings from Jaguar Cars to modify his 2.4 saloon to competition standard, and get the apprentices to do the modifications at his expense! He also instituted a number of other, at the time, quite revolutionary ideas in the sales team.

Due to the experimental nature of some parts, delays in production began to occur and the target for a record attempt of August 1960 had to be put back one month. As the car neared completion we were advised that Prince

HRH the Duke of Edinburgh inspecting CN7 with Ken and Lew Norris and DMC. (Rubery Owen Archive)

Philip, the Duke of Edinburgh, was interested in seeing it. Preparations for his visit, including a specially-constructed toilet close to the workshop just in case it was needed, further delayed completion.

Leo Villa had, during his years as a racing mechanic with Sir Malcolm Campbell, developed the ability to 'cat nap' whilst sitting on the concrete floor with his back to a wall. He would do this throughout the day whenever he wasn't needed – even for as little as 10 minutes. The rest of the team, however, couldn't do this and were becoming very tired indeed.

Leo and I had a major set-to when the engine was delivered from Bristol-Siddeley on May 11th. The lorry arrived at about 4pm, and it was decided that the engine should be fitted straight away. It just slipped into position and was connected to the driveshafts, when Leo said he wanted it taken out again. I questioned

Bluebird CN7

why that was necessary and was told that he needed to be sure about everything in case it was necessary when runs were being attempted. He would not listen to the argument that, if this was necessary, it would be the end of the attempt. I later realised that engine removal had been commonplace with Sir Malcolm's cars, and Leo would not accept that this was a totally different vehicle. He insisted on assembly and removal three more times that night, and we finally finished

The BP team practising refuelling on dummy Bluebird. (BP Archive)

at 4am! Needless to say the engine was never removed, other than after the Bonneville crash. It's worth noting here that every part of CN7 was designed to aircraft standards, with nothing left to 'fiddle fit,' something Leo was used to having to do in the past. He was undoubtedly a fantastic mechanic, but this project was beyond his knowledge. No doubt it was as a result of this that I was left out of the team for Utah!

At the same time as CN7 was being built, BP commissioned two long wheelbase Land Rover support vehicles, a fire tender, and two refuelling bowsers designed by Dave Harpum of the Norris team. The two support vehicles were equipped with hydraulic winches, long range fuel tanks, air compressors, generators, alternators,

electro-hydraulic power packs, and intercom radios. They also had extendible awnings on each side and at the rear, plus double skin 'tropical roofs' to protect the crews from the high temperatures of the salt flats. All of these were equipped by the Tooley Electro-Mechanical Co Ltd.

The Rover Company also supplied two long wheelbase Land Rovers to act as team transporters and a 3-litre Rover saloon for DMC's personal transport. At the end of each run the Land Rover tenders had to remove and replace the hot oil in the two transmission boxes, blow cooling air over the brakes, supply pressure for the inbuilt jacks for the tyre changes, recharge the compressed air braking system to 4000lb/in^2 (1814kg/ft^2) and charge the engine batteries for re-starting, all in about 30 minutes. The bowsers were 30cwt vans each holding 50 gallons (227 litres) of aviation fuel.

This project also led to us designing the first go-kart for BP. Powered by a lawnmower engine, it was great fun testing it on a disused RAF runway, doing 60mph with your bottom only 2in (5cm) from the tarmac.

The Campbell-Norris 7 with the first go-kart. (Rubery Owen Archive)

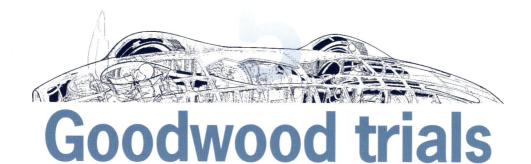

Goodwood trials

The team really came together when CN7 arrived at Goodwood race circuit during the night of Sunday 17th July 1959, and was unloaded from its transporter at about 10am on the 18th. Goodwood was to provide the arena for the car's press and public début, but we had not managed to test it in any way beforehand. Although CN7 could not build up any real speed at such a venue, it gave the team an opportunity to test all of the systems, practice wheel changes, etc, and for DMC to familiarise himself with driving the car. Before unloading, a chalk mark was made on each tyre where the wheel centre-line cut the trailer bed, and its location checked after rolling down the ramp. This was done to check transmission wind-up, which proved negligible. By 3pm CN7 was ready to be towed around the circuit with one of the Land Rover support vehicles as tug and another as anchor, attached to the fore and aft towing eyes. Many years later at a meeting at the National Motor Museum, Beaulieu to celebrate Ken's life, Richard Noble said in a speech: "Ken told me that he had a frightful night just before Campbell's great PR début with the CN7 Bluebird at Goodwood." This was to be the first time the CN7 would run under its own power, but the schedule had got so extended that the first taxi run had to be before the media. "I felt absolutely sure," he said in the inimitable Ken Norris way, "that it would run backwards, and I

BP advertisement for press launch. The author has the receding hairline on the far right of the picture. (BP Archive)

couldn't persuade myself otherwise." For the record, the beautiful car did run forward.

Ken was not the only one worried; all of us that had been involved with the design felt the same! However,

Bluebird CN7

CN7 being towed to check systems before starting the engine.
The author is on the left, shouting to Donald Campbell.
(BP Archive)

imagine our horror at the sound of 'tinkling' and of regular metallic 'clunks' as she moved forward! It took what seemed to be a lifetime, but was probably only a matter of seconds before we realised that the former was the turbine blades moving in their mounts and the latter was created by the disc brakes taking up the clearance on their support webs, both of which would disappear when the engine was fired up and the car on the move at speed. The clearances were necessary to allow for expansion in their mountings when the turbine blades were subjected to gas at 300°C, and in the brake discs when they were applied at high speed.

At about a third of the way around the course, the gearboxes were filled with oil and the tow proceeded at about 10-15mph (16-24kph). Lap speed, excluding the stop, was calculated to be 11.5mph (18.5kph) not 80mph (129kph) as I have seen reported elsewhere. DMC reported everything satisfactory, with the handling "exceptionally good" and corners turned with ease.

Engine start up. (Author's Collection)

Lineup of land speed record cars from the National Motor Museum. (Author's Collection)

DMC with Tonia after the first run at Goodwood. (BP Archive)

Bluebird CN7 touring Goodwood. The author and Hugh Standing are on the back of the Land Rover. (BP Archive)

Jack Brabham examining the cockpit at Goodwood with Tonia and DMC looking on. (BP Archive)

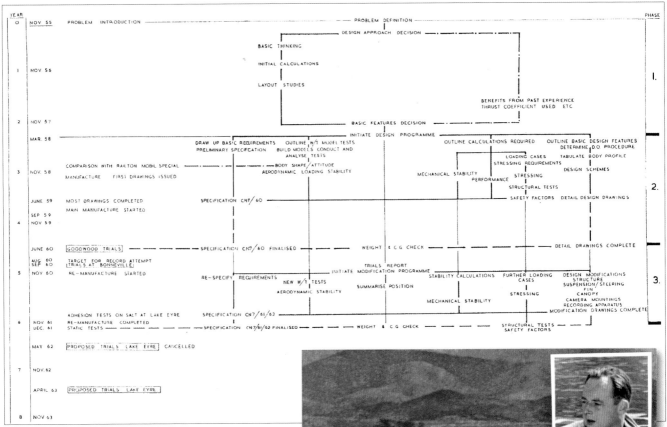

Project development flow chart. (Bluebird Trust)

Two static engine runs and systems checks were carried out in the hangar on the 20th, lasting 30 seconds and 100 seconds respectively. Slight buckling of the skin and paint scorching was noted. The next day longer runs of 3 and 6 minutes were made on the tarmac, with the same problems showing. On the 21st, the first 'free' run was completed with the following fire tender recording speeds of between 10 and 48mph (16-77kph). Air brakes were extended 'for practice only' when the pit area was reached. Three further uneventful runs were made on the 22nd, the second covering two laps in 19min, and reportedly reaching 100mph (161kph) on the straight. I seem to remember that the lap speed was about 60mph (96kph). Not much compared with a Grand Prix car, but with only 4 degrees of steer, corners had to be negotiated very slowly, and the car was designed to go in a straight line not around a circuit. For the third run, Peter Carr, the reserve driver, had his first, and only, drive. (I believe Peter can claim to be the only person to drive the car and not crash it!) Our concern regarding overheating of the adhesive in the area of the exhausts proved unfounded when the car was on the move, even at low speed. Following the press launch

DMC's presentation to Peter Carr after the record attempt at Lake Mead. (Peter Carr Collection)

the car stayed at Goodwood until the 22nd whilst further tests and familiarisation practices took place.

Whilst Ken became involved in the testing and operation of the Campbell-Norris 7, Lew took the lead in other areas of business, a vital task which kept money-making projects going so that the company could survive. He was particularly responsible for the Worcester Valve Co, Norco Engineering, and various other design and manufacturing projects.

Utah runs and crash

September 1st saw the team staying in the Western Motel, Wendover, Utah; with CN7 at the USAF base some 12 miles (19km) from the salt flats. Squadron Leader Peter Carr, the reserve driver, had spent time in the US before retiring from the RAF, and had contacts at a senior level in the USAF which enabled this to be arranged. It had been planned that I would be part of the team, and I was written into the script for the film being produced by David Cobham of RHR Productions for BP. However, my altercation with Leo over the engine installation meant that I was 'persona non grata!'

When Ken Norris returned to the office after the crash, our first task was to amalgamate his notes, data and memories into a single document. My copy of that document is the most effective description of what happened at Bonneville, and is reproduced 'in toto' in the following pages. I stress that this is a carbon copy of the original typed version and is possibly the only one remaining. It also includes brief notes on the earlier trials at Goodwood. A 'tarted up' version with some changes was later produced by 'Roneo' in a more suitable form for issuing to the companies that had participated in the project.

Relevant photographs, which were not included in the report, and some notes by me, have been placed after the report.

Report begins on following page. Main text continues on page 104.

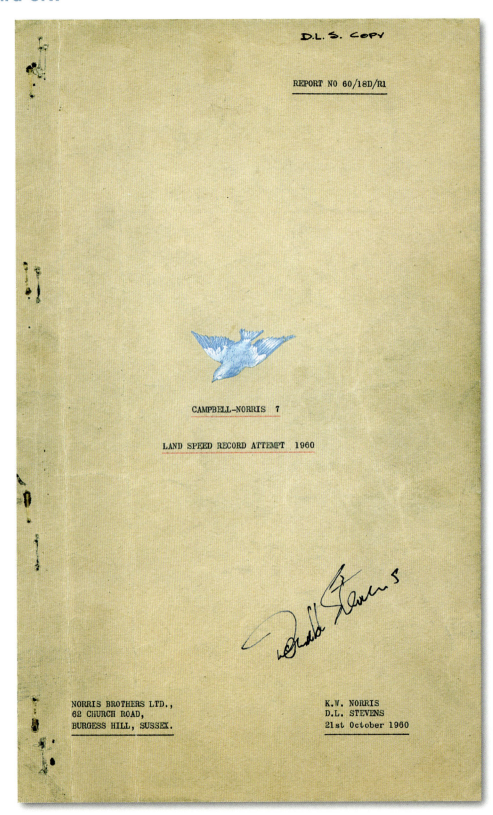

D.L.S. COPY

REPORT NO 60/18D/R1

CAMPBELL-NORRIS 7

LAND SPEED RECORD ATTEMPT 1960

NORRIS BROTHERS LTD.,
62 CHURCH ROAD,
BURGESS HILL, SUSSEX.

K.W. NORRIS
D.L. STEVENS
21st October 1960

C O N T E N T S

13 12 19 25

Bluebird CN7

1.	Runs 1 & 2	Bonneville Salt Flats Monday 5.9.60

(i) General

A final check up on the car in the workshop was made between 8.45 a.m. and 10.30 a.m. At 10.30 a.m. the team retired to the Western Motel for a general discussion re the trials programme for the immediate future runs. It was agreed to try Run 1 at a constant compressor r.p.m. of 6,500 and then, all being well, to increase the c r.p.m. to 7,000 for Run 2. No turning was to be done until the tyres had been thoroughly examined by Dunlops. As difficulty was expected in obtaining telemetred readings and R.T. readings from D.M.C., owing to transmission difficulties on the flats, the only data asked for was speed at the end of the first $\frac{1}{2}$ mile, maximum speed and feel from the driver in addition to the readings from the timekeeper and U.S.A.C.

Loading of the car onto the trailer commenced at noon and the complete caravan of transporter, landrovers (with ancilliary equipment) and rover cars (team) arrived on the flats (after a short stop for lunch) at 1.30 p.m. Unloading Bluebird, positioning, changing wheels and tyres etc. took approximately $2\frac{1}{2}$ hours so that all was ready for starting at approximately 4.0 p.m.

On initially starting a stream of overflow engine oil was discharged from the overboard bleed on the port underside, presumably owing to over filling. This made things very difficult for Dunlops as the oil was immediately in front of the rear tyres. Sacks were used in an attempt to shield the tyres and soak up the oil. On attempting to cut the engine nothing happened; the engine just kept on running much to everyone's consternation, as after a few minutes things were getting very hot at the aft end. Eventually Mr. Reakes discovered that the master switch was not 'ON' and hence the electrical circuits were not energised. A restart with 'CUT' indicated that all was well. Unfortunately, on starting again for Run 1 insufficient time had elapsed and a 'BOOM' of a wet start resulted in a minor fire taking place at the rear gear box compartment. (It was later discovered that sudden expansion had buckled the inner skin of the top gear box cover and had broken it free from the reduxing. However, the fire soon stopped and Run 1 commenced.

(ii) Run 1. South to North. Start approx. 5.35 p.m.

This commenced at a leisurely rate but acceleration increased steadily and the rover cars following were soon left way behind (at around 70 m.p.h.) Acceleration appeared to be very smooth and the car quite straight running and steady. On arrival at the north end the car was stopped facing north for tyre examination prior to turnaround.

D.M.C. appeared quite happy and stated that the acceleration was "fantastic!" Apparently the idling c.r.p.m. was only 4,000 and it had been necessary to increase c.r.p.m. up to 8,000 where it was held. Steering appeared to be somewhat direct. Slowing procedure had been throttle back, unwind, cut, airbrakes out, mechanical brakes on. As far as D.M.C. could tell, his peak speed had been 150 m.p.h. (subsequently the speed average through the mile was given as approximately 120 m.p.h.) The tyres appeared to K. W. Norris to be quite cool but D. Badger of Dunlops insisted that they were really quite warm for such a slow speed run. On taking off the rear gear box cover both underside of cover and most of the upper part of the compartment were seen to be covered in soot.

(ii) Run 1 – contd.

Checking oil temperature (engine), recharging air bottles and topping up fuel tanks etc. took approximately 35 minutes. A wait of 20 minutes occured, however, before the track was cleared for Run 2.

(iii) Run 2. North to South.   Start approx. 6.42 p.m.

As the car was facing North, after starting the engine, the car pulled away fairly soon onto a wide L.H. turn to bring it back onto the track going South. Acceleration was somewhat more rapid than Run 1 and the Rover cars following at 90 m.p.h. were soon left behind. On arrival at the South end D.M.C. turned slightly to starboard and brought the car round on a L.H. turn to stop at approximately 45° to the course c.l. Stopping procedure had apparently been to cut enging $\frac{3}{4}$ mile from the end of the mile, air brakes out, mechanical brakes on $\frac{1}{2}$ mile from stop. The compressor had been wound up to 8,300 r.p.m. and peak speed probably 180 m.p.h. The timekeepers' approx. check was 170 average through the mile. Tyres according to D. Badger were cooler than for Run 1.

(iv) Surface conditions (Nationals course used)

These were not good. The course was limited to about 11 miles and was somewhat patchy with potholes up to $\frac{1}{2}$" deep 6" across and large cracks in parts 1" deep, 2-3" across running along and across the course. Crack patterns ranged from 6 to 8 ft. longitudinal pitch to up to 30ft. longitudinal pitch. In general, where the patterns were small the cracks were narrower and less deep. The crack pattern was accompanied by a dishing at the centre of the pattern and this was not always removed by scraping particularly for the smaller patterns. (see sketch opposite).

(v) Remarks

(a)   Gear box circulating pumps were run for approximately 15 minutes prior to Run 1.

(b)   It was not considered necessary to change the engine oil after Run 1 as this was quite cool 66.5°C.

(c)   Plenum chamber pressure at the end of Run 1 was 0.5 lb/sq.in. At the end of Run 2 the gauge indicated zero pressure – this needs investigation.

(vi) Meeting following Runs 1 and 2

After Runs 1 and 2 a general meeting was held (6.9.60) to discuss the results and the future programme. As regards the latter, prior to further runs it was decided to:-

(a)   Change the steering ratio to 100:1 (D.M.C. request).

(b)   Instal warning light to indicate car electrical supply on.

(c)   Pad all projections in the cockpit.

(d)   Put blade under heel of throttle foot and pad at toe.

(e)   Carry out engine test run to set idling, which appeared to have altered to 4,500 c.r.p.m.

(f)   Carry out weight check.

(vi)   Meeting following Runs 1 and 2 (contd.)

    (g)   Fit fuel cut-off for use in emergency.

    (h)   Shield underside of top rear gear box cover and tighten
          turbine casing/trouser joint ring.

2.   Static Engine Test 1 – 11.9.60   (fuel cut-off cock and main SW warning
                                     light fitted)

This test was carried out on the apron in front of the hanger.
The object of the test was to

(i)   (a)   Set idling c.r.p.m. to 6,500.

    (b)   Check for oil leaks.

    (c)   To familiarise D.M.C. with cockpit drill.

    (d)   To check steering wheel feel at the same time.

(ii)   The engine started quite sell, but with a fair amount of flame
from the exhaust. After a short while oil dripped from both the
common overboard bleed and from the engine intake guard. No
covers were fitted and it was apparent from the oil on the ground
that the oil dripping from the guard had passed through the engine,
presumably the rear compressor bearing. No oil appeared to be
coming from the rear turbine bearing, confirming the belief that
this only occurs when the engine is cut during runs and there is
then no pressure for the air seal. Oil was apparently being burnt
off the trousers, causing a considerable amount of smoke. This
oil was probably the result of engine cut during Runs 1 and 2.
On examination of the rear turbine bearing after the test a small
amount of oil had still apparently leaked. The structure around
the exhaust system was quite cool even after 7 minutes running,
indicating that the exhaust shields are quite satisfactory. A
reading of 40°C. in the rear compartment was obtained from telemetry.
Telemetry AC tacho appeared O.K. but D.M.C. had no reading. Telemetry
thermocouples appeared to be wired incorrectly.

(iii)   Conclusions

    (a)   It was not possible to set the idling c.r.p.m. as the take
         up had insufficient travel.

    (b)   There are two main oil leaks apart from the overboard drain,
         i.e. the rear compressor bearing and the rear turbine bearing
         regions. The leaks we may have to 'live' with and take care
         of the oil against fire risk. The overboard drain trouble may
         require attention to careful quantity filling and pump pressures.
         Some of the trouble may be due to pushing the car backwards.

3.   Static Engine Test 2.   6.55 p.m. 12.9.60   (more idling adjustment provided)

(i)   This test again carried out on the apron in front of the hanger.

    Objects:-

    (a)   To set idling c.r.p.m.

    (b)   To check for oil leaks.

Static Engine Test 2 (contd.)

(ii) The engine started quite well, but oil began to leak from the
connection to the oil pressure check gauge and the engine had
to be cut after about ½ minute.

4. Static Engine Test 3. 7.13 p.m. 12.9.60 (connection tightened)

(i) Objects as above for Test 2.

(ii) The engine started well and was run for about 6 minutes.
The idling c.r.p.m. was set at about 6,500 and no oil leaks
were apparent.

The structure around the exhaust system remained remarkably cool,
until the engine was cut, indicating that the new lagged shields
were very effective.

This run is the most successful engine run to date and everyone
is quite happy for the car trials to resume.

Ref. form for further details of engine runs.

5. Runs 3 and 4   Bonneville Salt Flats Thursday 15.9.60

(Notes made 7.10.60 on return to England)

(i) General

The ten-day period following runs 1 and 2 and subsequent to runs
3 and 4 was filled with activity in the workshop. The change in
steering ratio from 25:1 to 100:1 occupied 5 to 6 days of this
period as it was necessary to completely remove the instrument
panel, wiring, etc. On re-assembling the panel, all instruments
were face mounted to make things easier. Sponge rubber padding
was placed in the cockpit over all projections, under lower edge
of instrument panel etc. and the cockpit made more comfortable
generally. The steering transducer was secured to the bulkhead
aft of the seat and the track rod cover cut away to receive the
mechanism. Collimated instrument glass screen was cut to about
a 4" wide strip across. A 1" bore Worcester valve was fitted to
the low pressure fuel line (before the low pressure pump) as an
emergency cut off, operated from the cockpit via a Bowden cable.
All was now set for an engine test run to set the idling etc.
This was carried out at 6.00 a.m. (11.9.60) on the apron in front
of the hangar. Oil leaks were discovered from the engine air
intake and the common drain (ref. Static Engine Test Notes 12.9.60).
It was not possible to set the idling owing to limitation of the
screw setting and a further test was suggested for the following day.
Engine test run 2 was carried out at about 7.00 p.m. on the 12th,
but the engine had to be cut owing to a leak as a result of not
correcting the engine oil pressure check gauge correctly. This
was soon righted and engine test run 3 was very successful. Only
8 gallons of oil had been put in the engine oil system and no leaks
were seen anywhere. Idling c.r.p.m. was set at 6,500 r.p.m. and
all that remained to be done was a final check all round prior to
runs 3 and 4. Unfortunately this final check showed that the
steering suspension geometry was such that the wheels were toed
out on rebound and toed in on bump, owing to the track rod link
operating through a different part of the arc to the wishbones.
Panic stations were organised and the runs contemplated for the
following day were cancelled. The next two days were largely

FITTING

Runs 3 and 4 (contd.)

devoted to modifying the hub/steering arm attachment to bring the track rod steering link into line with the wishbones so that the front wheels stayed in line. At 6.00 p.m. on the 14th this was completed.

All was now ready for Run 3 and it was agreed at a meeting on the morning of the 15th that Run 3 should be run at a c.r.p.m. of 7,500 and all being well Run 4 at 8,500 c.r.p.m.

(ii)   Run 3.   South to North.   Start approx. 4.30 p.m. 15.9.60

This went off quite smoothly, starting at 7,000 c.r.p.m. and building up to 7,500 c.r.p.m. The main comments by D.M.C. at the end of the run were as follows:-

(a)   Speed at 1 mile   – 100 m.p.h.
      Speed at 5 miles   – 165 m.p.h.
      Max. speed at 6 miles   – 175 m.p.h.

(b)   Air brakes out 175 m.p.h.

(c)   No deceleration until brakes on and engine cut.

(d)   Steering – "like Chevrolet" – no feel.

(e)   Car dancing up and down – course bad.

(f)   3 applications of mechanical brakes made. Mechanical brakes O.K.

At the end of Run 3 the rear brakes were much hotter than the front (may be due to exhaust heat). Front brakes were cool to hands – rear brakes hot, say 45°C. It was not necessary to change engine or gear box oil for Run 4. As the car was facing away from the course D.M.C. drove the car round and straight off for Run 4.

(iii)   Run 4.   North to South.   Start approx. 5.17 p.m. 15.9.60

This again went off quite smoothly apart from a cough from the engine coupled with a belch from the exhaust a short distance up the course. C.r.p.m. at the start was 8,500 as arranged but this built up to 10,000 during the run. Main comments by D.M.C. at the end of the run were as follows:-

(a)   Speed at 1 mile   – 150 m.p.h.
      Max. speed at 6 miles   – 240 m.p.h.

(b)   Air brakes out – 210 m.p.h.

(c)   Speed came off O.K. on throttling back and at 7 miles 100 lb/sq.in. brake pressure applied and engine cut.

(d)   Steering – car "wanders as an American car wanders going fast" (wind may do this)

(e)   "Can feel wheels gyrating from side to side. Wheels do not 'lock on' now".

Brake temperatures at the end of Run 4 were guessed at 240°C. rear and 180°C. front. Telemetry reported front off side suspension lower than rest after Run 3 but this was checked by removing wheel and taking measurements and appeared O.K. Steering hardly moved at all. The rear end of the car at the end of each run appeared to be quite cool.

Runs 3 and 4 (contd.)

   (iv) <u>Surface Conditions</u> (Nationals course used – 11½ miles approx.)

Conditions had improved since Runs 1 and 2 but nothing had been
done to the course subsequent to Mickey Thompson's run of 406.6 m.p.h.
(South to North) on Friday the 9th. From mile 0 to mile 1 going
South to North, the course was breaking up somewhat into potholes,
the largest of these being approximately 4ft. x 2ft. x 3 inches deep,
filled with loose salt, slightly to the right hand of the middle black
line and slightly South of mile 1.

<u>NOTE</u> The course had one central black oil line and one oil line
each side at 40ft. approximately from the centre, marking the edge
of the prepared salt region. Although the course is therefore 80ft.
wide, only the right hand side going South to North had been prepared
by grading and sweeping by M. Thompson's group.

  (v) <u>Remarks</u>

In general, Runs 3 and 4 were quite satisfactory. Some attention
to the steering was clearly required but did not appear necessary
before Run 5 as D.M.C. was not adamant (as he had been about changing
the 25:1 ratio) that he was very concerned.

  (vi) <u>Meeting following Runs 3 and 4</u>

This was held the same evening at about 8.45 p.m. D.M.C's comments
on the runs were that the car tended to veer to the West during
Run 3 and that it drifted to the West about 5ft. from the centre
line during Run 4. It had been necessary to make three corrections
at approximately $\pm 10^{\circ}$ steering wheel angle during Run 4. The
wheels appeared to be toeing in and out when NOT steering. Mechanical
brakes were very good. There did not appear to be two complete turns
of steering wheel lock to lock.

In preparation for Run 5 contemplated the next morning, it was agreed:-

(a)   To check the steering lock to lock.

(b)   To run at 9,000/9,500 c.r.p.m. up to 300 m.p.h.

D.M.C. indicated that he would like to come down from 300 m.p.h.
in minimum distance and further would like to do a maximum
acceleration check. The latter did not receive approval generally
but no bar was definitely imposed.

Pressure readings were asked for from cockpit instruments,
but D.M.C. said this was not possible owing to concentration
on steering. There seemed to be an inherent error of cockpit
to DIDAS speed readings. Alan Potton reported that he knew of
a 5% error and this was left for later discussion.

The wind during Run 3 had gusted from 3 to 5 p.m. from East;
during run 4 up to 10 m.p.h. from East. This could account
for concentration required on steering.

6.   Runs 5 and 6   Bonneville Salt Flats Friday 16.9.60

(i) General

No changes were contemplated following Runs 3 and 4 and prior
to Run 5. An early morning start was agreed and the car, which
had returned to the hangar for the night after Run 4 was on the
flats by 4.30 a.m. By 6.0 a.m. all was ready for Run 5.
Steering had been checked lock to lock by Leo Villa and K. W. Norris
and check measurements made on suspension position (wheels off).
All was well and Run 5 commenced after D.M.C. had inspected the
pothole close to mile 1 with Tommy Wisdom and K. W. Norris.

(ii) Run 5. South to North.   Start approx. 6.22 a.m.

Wind was gusting 3 to 6 m.p.h. from SSE as the car was wound
up to 9,500 c.r.p.m. and D.M.C. pulled away well to the right hand
of the central black line to miss the pothole at mile 1.
Ambient temperature was almost $17^{\circ}C.$, so good engine performance
was expected.

D.M.C's comments at the end of the run were as follows:-

(a)   Speed at end of 3 miles - 300 m.p.h.
       (K. W. Norris reminded D.M.C. that 300 m.p.h. was required
       in 2 miles for record).

(b)   C.r.p.m. up to 10,000+

(c)   Stopping procedure. Engine cut - air brakes out - foot
       brakes on 120 lb/sq.in. at $7\frac{1}{2}$ mile mark - speed down from
       260 to 95 m.p.h. in 3 miles. Mechanical brakes were very
       good indeed.

(d)   Jet pipe temperature reached $600^{\circ}C.$ max.

(e)   Steering was light and car wanted to wander off.

In general, everyone was very happy with the run. Gear box and
engine oil temperature did not indicate necessity to change oil.
The car was turned round by hand (to prevent peculiar bias to
fuel system evident from Run 4 when fuel was used more from
starboard tank than port) and placed with the right hand wheels a
few feet from the black line in the left hand lane of course,
facing South.

D.M.C. again requested that during Run 6 he should try both the
acceleration of the car and also braking hard at the other end.
After consultation with Leo Villa and Don Badger (Dunlops) this
was agreed, but as the air brakes had not had their static land
test and only 300 m.p.h. tyres were fitted, a top speed limit
of 300 m.p.h. was imposed. After Run 6 it was agreed, all being
well, that the air brake test should be carried out in the
afternoon, adjustments should be made to give the front wheels
"toe out" (to compare with Runs 1 and 2) and then the 400 m.p.h.
tyres would be fitted for Run 7. Also consideration should be
given to locking the cross differentials and replacing the free
wheel front shaft with the "solid" drive, it being agreed between
D. Badger and K. W. Norris that this was probably best.

(iii) Run 6. North to South. Start approx. 7.10 a.m. 16.9.60

C.r.p.m. was built up to 9,500 with static as for Run 5. Leo Villa
closed the canopy and gave the thumbs up sign. K. W. Norris standing
nearby almost decided to tap on the canopy and to warn D.M.C. to keep

Run 6 (contd.)

clear of the black line but all was set to go and at this stage
might be confusing. As C.N.7 pulled away at a very smart pace,
K. W. Norris knelt down to note tyre to salt adhesion. There
appeared to be no slip and all was well. Wind was gusting up to
8 m.p.h. from SSE.

About 1.6 miles (i.e. 1.5 miles from mile 0, there being 0.1 miles
from mile 0 to the start of the run) up the course, C.N.7 started
to go off track finishing nearly broadside on at 1.9 miles in a
spiral left hand slide. From then on the car took off for nearly
200 yards bouncing several times before coming to rest approximately
500 yards away on the salt to the left of the course and into wind.

This final run may perhaps be best described in the first person,
as follows:-

"7.10 a.m. and as C.N.7 pulled away it was obvious that she was
accelerating very fast and Leo and I made a quick dash for our
Rover follow-up car which was parked about 20 yards away facing
the course. We were quickly up to 90 m.p.h. on the right hand
side of the right hand marker line but C.N.7 was by then a speck
on the horizon. Suddenly, there appeared to be more "dust" than
usual surrounding C.N.7 and then from this cloud a blue object
flew upwards. My immediate thought was that the top plenum chamber
cover had flown off and I cursed inwardly for not doing more stringent
tests. My immediate reaction that the Skipper would be O.K. if it
was indeed the top cover was quickly dispelled as the cloud had now
increased considerably and appeared to be way to the left hand of
the course. Leo's comment was "My God, he's in trouble" and I
prayed "Please God, he's alright" as Leo plunged across the track
heading straight for the cloud.

We were doing a good 90 m.p.h. and it took us a mere 60 seconds
to reach what was left of the car, but those 60 seconds seemed
endless. The past kept imposing itself with endless accusations.
"You should have done this" and "that" and "that" !!

I don't remember anything of the wreckage on the way across the salt,
my eyes being fixed on the black blob ahead. As we drew near, it
seemed that C.N.7 was upside down and I felt sick and empty inside -
but closer still and it was apparent that she was the right way up
and as Leo was screeching to a halt I was preparing to jump from the
doorway. I could think of nothing but reaching the canopy and
yanking it up. I could see Donald's head nodding to and fro dazedly
inside the crash helmet, looking weird and ungainly. Another leap
and I yanked the canopy external release at the front end. A jump
and I was on the wreck at the back end trying to prise up the
perspex. Leo was now at the front and he pulled the release again
and the canopy came up easily.

Blood was spattered in places over the Skipper's blue overalls,
but he seemed O.K. otherwise. Consciousness of the engine running
sweetly impelled me to action again and I skipped down the far side
of the canopy and grabbed across the cockpit for the emergency fuel
cut-off. Nothing happened and Leo and I pulled on the release
together. The engine stopped and Peter Carr was leaning over the
far side of the cockpit to release the harness. Back behind the
Skipper and Tonia was running across the salt her legs dragging
slower and slower as she approached. Thumbs up and a short
"He's O.K." and she came on again as strong arms were dragging the
Skipper free. The ambulance was now alongside, the stretcher was
out and Tonia was hovering over the Skipper as he mumbled "I seem
to have clouted my ear" on his way to the ambulance.

Run 6 (contd.)

"Go away pressmen, can't you see he's hurt". No! we don't know
what's happened yet!!"

The ambulance pulled away and we gazed dumfounded at what a few
seconds past was to be the fastest car in the world. Dejection
follows as we wander slowly back through scattered wreckage to
the course and the start of the trouble.

The black line – "look, it all started at the black line!!"
"why in hell's name Leo did he go onto the black line?".

No jumping to conclusions – sanity returns as we pass pencil and
paper round to team members and outline a systematic combing of
the run right from the start.

Back at mile 0 minus .10 we spread out and advance slowly back up
the course measuring and inspecting carefully, paced by a Rover car.

The tracks of Run 6 appear not to the left hand of the course but
to the right hand, where there are brown sweepings of salt from
the left hand prepared side. This is not good surface and – look
now – the left hand wheel track is turning into two distinct tracks.
It looks as though a wheel may have been wobbling. Quickly measure
up the distance between tracks and pace up the course. It certainly
looks like a wheel wobble – those ball ends must have given – If
this is true he was really in trouble. But not the car has turned
into a three wheeler – thank God for that – that squashes the wheel
wobble theory. We must be confused with Run 5 tracks.

Further up the track and Leo postulates another theory – the car
must have taken off. No! that's definitely OUT!! The wheel
tracks now return for the second time towards the black line and
soon the left hand wheels are running entirely on the black line.
Here the line really is black as though all the salt covering has
been removed. 1.6 miles and the wheel tracks are turning left
and changing into two distinct tracks. 1.7 miles and the left hand
wheels are 20 inches to the left hand side of the black line and
rapidly fading in width and intensity, as load leaves the left hand
side of the car and bears down on the right hand side. 1.9 miles
and the right hand wheel tracks are wide and intense – all the load
has gone from the left hand side. Distance between the right hand
wheel track is now 11'2" and the car must have been almost broadside.
There is now a deep groove in the salt, possibly from the right hand
front wheel, followed by blue markings between the tracks and then
nothing!

The track is clear again for about 100 yards and there we have neatly
spaced all the wheel covers. Then nothing further, apart from three
heads and shanks of $\frac{1}{4}$" dia. bolts and one fastener, for a further
100 yards when we see that the tail end of the car has touched down.
A little further and the front has touched down hard! Did the
Skipper get his clout here?

Bits of rubber – a few more yards and blue marks from the length
of the body. Here we see the starboard front wheel fairing. And
then a 5/16" dia. washer and nut and a balance weight. A few more
paces and we find the front port wheel fairing.

My God it's hot, it's 12.30p.m. and I've forgotten to take off my
sweater! Can't stop now though – got to see this through.

More paces and another touch down, wheel rim marks and some more
nuts. Now we find some bits of honeycomb and some fastener pins.
A little further and the car has touched down once again; more
5/16" dia. wheel rim nuts; more $\frac{1}{4}$" dia. nuts; some honeycomb and

Run 6 (contd.)

a ring clip. 340 yards from the slide off and we find a steering arm bracket, some bits of hub seal and later one half shaft, in apparently good condition, deposited with the rear starboard wheel, complete with leg, steering arm and a huge hunk of main beam. Another 20 yards and he is the top front starboard wishbone, starboard leg and a piece of battery bakelite. Then a long sweeping slide for 100 yards across the salt to the wreck. In the distance 200-300 yards away we see the front starboard wheel.

Sandwiches and pop! Not much inclined - but perhaps I'd better!

2.00 p.m. and Peter Carr returns - the skipper's O.K., but has suspected skull fracture - murmers of relief!!

A crane has arrived and we watch quietly whilst the chains crunch into the aluminium sheet as the slack is taken up. Can't salvage much anyway - look along - the body is warped.

Not much more to be done here now. Better inspect that front starboard wheel and then get back to Wendover to telephone home."

At 3.30 p.m. the team meets in the hangar for a discussion and at 4.30 p.m. Peter Carr and K. W. Norris fly to Toulle Hospital to see D.M.C. and to get his comments.

(iv) D.M.C's comments   6.30 p.m. 16.9.60

The Skipper appeared to be reasonably O.K. and in a position to answer questions, so K. W. Norris asked him why he went to the right hand (West) side of the course and why on earth he went on to the black.

D.M.C. replied "I started off and the car drifted across to the right, I corrected once to the left and again the car drifted to the right; I corrected again to the left - noticed the needle passing the 300 m.p.h. mark and I told myself that I must correct carefully - and that's all I remember".

On further discussion D.M.C. indicated that he had wanted to get out of the car at the other end and be able to tell K. W. Norris that he's reached 300 m.p.h. easily in 2 miles. He was extremely sorry for messing things up for everybody!

(v)   Comments from Don Badger (Dunlop)

On being asked by K. W. Norris what he thought had happened Don Badger replied "It got away with him!".

7.   Reasons for the crash

The answer to the question "Why did the car leave the track?" is undoubtedly "Because the limiting tyre coefficient was exceeded!!"

The question "But why was the limiting tyre coefficient exceeded?" may be answered as follows:-

(a)   The limiting tyre coefficient was relatively low due to the poor condition of the salt over which the car was running particularly on the region of the black line.

7. **Reasons for crash (contd.)**

(b)   The output torque from the engine was higher than was anticipated, partly due to the peculiar torque characteristic with the C.N.7 exhaust arrangement, partly due to operation at 17°C. and partly due to lack of experience with this type of engine. Indeed the driver must have been surprised to find after selection of the throttle position that the torque "followed" up and hit him so hard!!

(c)   Some of the limiting tyre coefficient was used to make course correction into wind, leaving a lower margin for tractive effort.

(d)   The attention required by the driver to the steering must have detracted from other things, such as foot feel, demanding attention.

8. **Suggested modifications for rebuild of C.N.7**

(a)   Much stronger arrangements are required for holding the wheels in track. The evidence indicates that the hub steering arms were the first parts of the structure to fail leaving the wheels free to swing on their king pins, the rims biting into and destroying the main beam structure.

(b)   Make the ball joints of suspension etc. have a much better elastic characteristic, probably by increasing the size. These joints were a constant source of worry during the trials.

(c)   Re-consider the steering ratio to be used and make the ball screw such that load feed back from caster effects is easier.

(d)   Allow for more caster.

(e)   Have adjustment on hub arms so that geometry can be corrected for caster changes.

(f)   Consider use of forged inserts instead of separate brackets at concentrated load pick ups to honeycomb beams.

(g)   Have a much better throttle pedal linkage.

(h)   Sights to be fixed to FRONT end of car to give some idea to the driver of yaw of body.

(j)   Fit braking parachute which is tripped by a gyro when car yaws more than 2°.

(k)   Make suspension adjustment in wishbone arms not at ball ends.

(l)   Increase size of suspension leg pick-up beam insert.

(m)   Make stiffeners on face of main beam full depth from bottom bracket up to wishbone bracket stiffeners at either side.

(n)   CHANGE OVER POSITION OF FUEL TANKS & AIR BOTTLES

(o)   RE-CONSIDER FITTING AERODYNAMIC FIN & DESIGN REMOVABLE FIN

(p)   CONSIDER DRIVER PROTECTION & DESIGN TO SUIT.

9.   Suggestions for future trials

(a)   Do <u>Not</u> operate in any wind at all.

(b)   Make quite sure that the course is well prepared from surface and width point of view. The complete width of at least 80ft. should be graded and brushed.

(c)   The course should be marked with a black line either side only — i.e. there should be no oil line in the middle unless a black dye which does not harm the salt can be used.

(d)   Approach the high speeds with much more caution.

(e)   D.M.C. to study cockpit drill and course very much more.

(f)   Lock cross differentials.

(g)   Use fixed front drive shaft, i.e. no free wheel.

10.   Ambient Conditions 11.10.60

Discussion with Met. office at Wendover Base Box at 4240ft.

The low* temperature occurs between 4 and 7 a.m.

Temperature is then about   61°F. (16°C.)

The lowest evening temperature occurs at about 9.0 p.m. and is about   75°F. (24°C.)

Barometric Pressure is about   12.7 lb/sq.in.

*NOTE: the lowest temperature coincides with maximum humidity.

We are quite welcome to get readings anytime.

Barometric readings are in inches of mercury —

Conversion   29.9" = 760 m.m.   =   14.7 lb/in^2

Bluebird CN7

RUN No & DRIVER	LOCATION	DATE	TIME O'CLOCK	RUN DIRECTION	WIND M.P.H.	WIND DIRECTION	AMBIENT PRESSURE P.S.I.	AMBIENT TEMPERATURE °C	OFFICIAL TIME SECS	OFFICIAL SPEED M.P.H.	DURATION RUN MINS & SECS	DURATION ENGINE MINS & SECS	FUEL USED GALLS PORT	FUEL USED GALLS STARBOARD	RELATIVE HUMIDITY	OXYGEN (FULL)
							OBSERVATIONS									
MAX.	GOODWOOD						4228 FT						12½	12½		
—	TOWED RUN	18.7.60														
—	FIRST ENGINE RUN STATIC	20.7.60	6.40 6.48									.30 1.40				
D.MC/D.MC	STATIC	21.7.60	12.59 1.48									6.00 3.00	5			
1 D.MC	1 CIRCUIT	21.7.60	1.51						10 48		7.0	9.00				
2 D.MC	1 CIRCUIT	22.7.60	2.55						12 52		5.0	8.00	4	5		
3 D.MC	2 CIRCUIT	22.7.60	3.24						15 55		17.0	19.00	4	10		
4 P.C	1 CIRCUIT	22.7.60	4.54						—		7.0	8.00				
1	BONNEVILLE SALT FLATS	5.9.60	5.35 P.M	N	0	0	12.6	33	30	120	0.30 10.30	8.00 .30 12.40	6	6		
2	——"——	"	6.42 P.M	S	0	0	12.6	33	21	170	7.55	6.00	9	0		
—	WENDOVER ENGINE STATIC	10.9.60	6.45 a.m.		4,500 ft		127	21				7.00	5	5		
—	——"——	12.9.60	6.55 P.M				126	28.6				0.30			17%	
—	——"——	12.9.60										6.00				
3	SALT FLATS	15.9.60	4.30 P.M	N	5 TO 7	SE							6	5		
4	——"——	13.9.60	5.17 P.M	S	UP TO 10	SE							4	8		
5	——"——	16.9.60	6.22 a.m	N	3 TO 6	SSE		20 17				6.00	5	4		¾
6	——"——	16.9.60	7.10 a.m	S	8	SE		16.7			0.30	4.00				

LOCATION	RUN Nº	A.U.W. LBS.	C.G. POSITION. INS.	BALLAST LBS.	BALLAST POSITION	OIL GALLS. ENGINE	OIL GALLS. FRONT GEARBOX.	OIL GALLS. REAR GEARBOX.	FUEL GALLS. PORT.	FUEL GALLS. STARBOARD.	FUEL FLOW SETTING LBS/HOUR	FRONT SHAFT.	DIFFERENTIAL.	STEERING RATIO.	ENGINE GEARBOX POSITION.
GOODWOOD	MAX.					10	12	12	12½	12½					
TOWED RUN	—														
FIRST ENGINE RUN STATIC	—										2200				℄
STATIC	—										2200				℄
1 CIRCUIT	1	8670	-3.6	0	—	10	10	10	10	10	2200	F W	IN	25:1	℄
1 CIRCUIT	2	8670	-3.6	0	—	10	10	10			2200	F W	IN	25:1	℄
2 CIRCUIT	3	8670	-3.6	0	—	10	10	10			2200	F W	IN	25:1	℄
1 CIRCUIT	4	8670	-3.6	0	—	10	10	10			2200	F W	IN	25:1	℄
BONNEVILLE SALT FLATS	1	9150+	+2	224	+134	10	8	8	12½	12½	2200	F.W	IN	25:1	℄
— " —	2	9150+	+2	224	+134	10	8	8	12½	12½	2200	FW	IN	25:1	℄
WENDOVER ENGINE STATIC	—			224	+134	8	10	10	12½	12½	2200	FW	IN	100:1	℄
— " —	—			224	+134	7	10	10	12	12	2200	FW	IN	100:1	℄
— " —	—			224	+134	8	10	10	12	12	2200	FW	IN	100:1	℄
SALT FLATS	3			224	+134	7½	10	10	12	12	2200	FW	IN	100:1	℄
— " —	4			224	+134	7½	10	10	12	12	2200	FW	IN	100:1	℄
— " —	5			224	+134	7½	10	10	12	12	2200	FW	IN	100:1	℄
— " —	6			224	+134	7½	10	10	12	12	2200	FW	IN	100:1	℄

		CONFIGURATION																				
LOCATION	RUN No	TYRE PRESSURE P.S.I.		LEG PRESSURE P.S.I.		DAMPER SETTING		CASTOR INS.		TOE IN. INS.		CAMBER INS.		DRIVING FLANGE OFFSET INS		BODY CLEARANCE INS			HUB CONDITION LEG UP		SPACERS	
		F	R	F	R	F	R	F	R	F	R	F	R	F	R	+81	0	-81	F	R	F	R
GOODWOOD	MAX																					
TOWED RUN	–																					
FIRST ENGINE RUN STATIC	–																					
STATIC	–																					
1 CIRCUIT	1			950	950	DESIGN		0	0	0	0	0	0	3/8	1/8				L	L	1	1
1 CIRCUIT	2			950	950	DESIGN		0	0	0	0	0	0	3/8	1/8				L	L	1	1
2 CIRCUIT	3			950	950	DESIGN		0	0	0	0	0	0	3/8	1/8				L	L	1	1
1 CIRCUIT	4			950	950	DESIGN		0	0	0	0	0	0	3/8	1/8				L	L	1	1
BONNEVILLE SALT FLATS	1			950	950	DESIGN		1	0	0	0	0	0	3/8	1/8	5.5	4.9	5.6	L	L	1	1
—"—	2			950	950	DESIGN		1	0	0	0	0	0	3/8	1/8				L	L	1	1
WENDOVER ENGINE STATIC	–					DESIGN		1	0	0	0	0	0	3/8	1/8				L	L	1	1
—"—	–					DESIGN		1	0	0	0	0	0	3/8	1/8				L	L	1	1
—"—	–					DESIGN		1	0	0	0	0	0	3/8	1/8				L	L	1	1
SALT FLATS	3			950	950	DESIGN		1	0	0	1/16	0	0	3/8	1/8	5.75	5.1	6.3	L	L	1	1
—"—	4			950	950	DESIGN		1	0	0	1/16	0	0	3/8	1/8				L	L	1	1
—"—	5			950	950	DESIGN		1	0	0	1/16	0	0	3/8	1/8	5.63	5.0	5.88	L	L	1	1
—"—	6			950	950	DESIGN		1	0	0	1/16	0	0	3/8	1/8				L	L	1	1

LOCATION	RUN No.	TELEMETRY READINGS																		
		FRONT GEAR BOX				REAR GEAR BOX				ENGINE OIL PRESSURE P.S.I.	JET PIPE TEMP °C	COMPRESSOR R.P.M.	MAXIMUM SPEED M.P.H.	MAX. VERTICAL ACCELERATION G.	STEERING MOVEMENT IN THE MILE		SUSPENSION LEG. MAXIMUM DISPLACEMENT			
																	FRONT		REAR	
		CROWN WHEEL BEARING TEMP. °C	PINION BEARING TEMP. °C	OIL TEMP. °C	OIL PRESSURE P.S.I.	CROWN WHEEL BEARING TEMP. °C	PINION BEARING TEMP °C	OIL TEMP. °C	OIL PRESSURE P.S.I.						MAX. AMP. INS.	FREQUENCY C.P.M.	AMP. INS.	FREQUENCY C.P.M.	AMP. INS	FREQUENCY C.P.M.
GOODWOOD	MAX.	130	130	130	10	130	130	130	10	80	650	12,000	475	2.5						
TOWED RUN.	—																			
FIRST ENGINE RUN STATIC	—																			
STATIC	—																			
1 CIRCUIT	1																			
1 CIRCUIT	2																			
2 CIRCUIT	3	58	44	38																
1 CIRCUIT.	4																			
BONNEVILLE SALT FLATS	1																			
—	2																			
WENDOVER ENGINE STATIC	—	WRONG				WRONG						OK								
—	—											5000								
—	—											5500 7600								
SALT FLATS	3													±0.2*						
—	4										800 450	8500	250 265	±0.15*						
—	5																			
—	6												365	±0.3						

Bluebird CN7

LOCATION	RUN №	SUSPENSION ATTITUDE — ANALYSIS TAKEN FROM TELEMETRY RESULTS. SUSPENSION LEG MEAN DISPLACEMENT FROM STATIC POSITION ~ INS.															
		MAXIMUM SPEED				THROTTLE OPEN				THROTTLE CLOSED				ENGINE CUT			
		FP	FS	RP	RS	FP	FS	RP	RS	FP	FS	RP	RS	FP	FS	RP	RS
GOODWOOD.	MAX																
TOWED RUN.	—																
FIRST ENGINE RUN STATIC	—																
STATIC	—																
1 CIRCUIT																	
1 CIRCUIT																	
2 CIRCUIT.																	
1 CIRCUIT.																	
BONNEVILLE SALT FLATS	1																
— . —	2																
WENDOVER ENGINE STATIC	—																
— . —	—																
— .. —	—																
SALT FLATS	3																
— . —	4																
— .. —	5																
— .. —	6																

CAR INSTRUMENT READINGS.

LOCATION	RUN Nº	AIR BOTTLE PRESSURE P.S.I. A	B	P	AIR BRAKE	BRAKE PRESSURES P.S.I. A	B	P	F	R	GEAR BOX OIL PRESSURE P.S.I.	ENGINE OIL PRESSURE P.S.I.	FUEL MANIFOLD PRESSURE P.S.I.	COMPRESSOR DELIVERY PRESSURE P.S.I.	COMPRESSOR R.P.M.	JET PIPE TEMP °C	AIR BRAKE POSITION DEGREES	MAX. SPEED M.P.H.	MAX. ACCELERATION	MAX. DECELERATION	PLENUM CHAMBER PRESSURE P.S.I.	SPEED AT END MILE I.M.P.H.
GOODWOOD	MAX	3000	3000	3000	3000	260	260	300	10	10	80				9500	650						
TOWED RUN	—																					
FIRST ENGINE RUN STATIC	—														5800	600/480						
STATIC	—																					
1 CIRCUIT	1																					
1 CIRCUIT	2	270	260	340					7.0	8.0	60	150	120		6400	500						
2 CIRCUIT	3								9.5	9.5	60	150			5,400	550						
1 CIRCUIT	4	290	295	300					8.0	8.5	60					570						
BONNEVILLE SALT FLATS	1	2000	2200	1900	1900	260	290	295	8	8	40⊕	5	30/25		4000/8000	520/400	80	150			0·5	
"	2	2000	2000	2000	2000	260	260	280	8	8				100	8300		80	180			0	
WENDOVER ENGINE STATIC	—	1500	300	1500		260		300	8	4+				100	5200/8400	465/500						
"	—	2150	2050	1800	2150			290	8	8	10				5000	480						
"	—								8	8	66/100			110	5600/8000/6500	550/580						
SALT FLATS	3	2500	2700	2500	2500	300	300	300	8~	8~					7000/7500		80	165/175			0·25	100/1
"	4 2nd	2400	2200	2150	1900	300	300	300	7½	7½					8500/10000	540	80	240			0·10	150/1
"	5	2500/2400	2400/2000	2600/2000	2590/2000	320	300	300	8	6				220	9500/10000+	600	80	300			0·5	300/3
"	6	2500	2500	2400	2500	320	320	300	8~	8~	50				9500/10000+	540/525/560			350			

⊕ MOTORING CYCLE IN WORKSHOP 3·9·60.

Bluebird CN7

LOCATION	RUN Nº	ENGINE OIL TEMP °C	BEAM FACE REAR WHEEL BAY °C	BEAM FACE TELEMETRY COMPARTMENT °C	OUTSIDE SKIN OVER TURBINE °C	OUTSIDE SKIN – FORWARD END – TOP JET PIPES °C	OUTSIDE SKIN – MINOR AXIS TOP JET PIPE °C	BEAM FACE TELEMETRY COMP I TELEMETRY READING	AVERAGE CALIPER TEMP. °C	DISC BRAKE AIR DUCT MESH °C	REAR GEARBOX – COVER OVER TURBINE	REAR GEARBOX – COVER UNDER TURBINE	AUX. BEAM FACE ADJACENT TO UNLAGGED EXHAUST	ENTRY OF LAGGED EXHAUST INTO BEAMS	TUBULAR EXHAUST SHROUDS	AUX BEAM FACE ADJACENT TO AIR BRAKE ACCUMS.	MAIN BEAM – WHEEL BAY	REFRASIL LAGGING AROUND TROUSERS	STRUCTURE GENERALLY IN REAR GEARBOX COMPARTMENT.
GOODWOOD	MAX.																		
TOWED RUN	–																		
FIRST ENGINE RUN STATIC	–																		
STATIC	–																		
1 CIRCUIT	1		46			66													
1 CIRCUIT	2		50	45	55	85	85		133										
2 CIRCUIT	3	80	67		72	78				FEEL 90									
1 CIRCUIT	4																		
BONNEVILLE SALT FLATS	1	66.5									LOCAL 310	OK	155	310 / 155	67	OK	310	67	
— " —	2	74									310	OK	155	310 / 155	67	OK	310	67	
WENDOVER ENGINE STATIC	–							40									93~		
— " —	–																		
— " —	–																		
SALT FLATS	3	54						SOAK 40											
— " —	4	74																	
— " —	5	56																	
— " —	6																		

LOCATION	RUN No	SURFACE CONDITIONS	REMARKS
			TEMP. PAINT. BRONZE GREEN 150°C FIRST APPLICATION DEEP PURPLE BROWN 240°C R. GOVIER 2·9·60 PALE INDIAN RED 310°C
GOODWOOD	MAX		
TOWED RUN.	—		
FIRST ENGINE RUN STATIC	—		
STATIC	—		
1 CIRCUIT	1	RELATIVELY BUMPY COMPARED	BATTERIES IN AFT POSITION REAR PANEL COMING OFF – REPLACED.
1 CIRCUIT	2	WITH SURFACE CONTEMPLATED	BATTERIES IN AFT POSITION.
2 CIRCUIT.	3	i.e. SALT FLATS	
1 CIRCUIT.	4		
BONNEVILLE SALT FLATS	1	11+ MILES CRACKS IN PLACES PATCHY NOT VERY GOOD YEAR.	THROTTLE MOVED TO 8000 CRPM & HELD AIR BOTTLE PRESSURE DROPPED 100LB A & B BACK THROTTLE UNWIND CUT AIR BRAKES.
———"———	2	———"———"———"———"———	NO ENGINE OIL CHANGE BRAKES ON ¾ MILE FROM END. CUT ¾ MILE FROM END OF MILE.
WENDOVER ENGINE STATIC	—	ON CONCRETE IN FRONT OF HANGAR OIL LEAKS – REAR COMP. BEARING & COMMON	ALL COVERS OFF – OIL BURNING OFF TROUSER DRAIN. NO LEAK – REAR TURBINE BEARING.
———"———	—	CONCRETE APRON FRONT OF HANGAR.	OIL LEAK FROM TEST ENGINE PRESSURE GAUGE CONNECTION
———"———	—	———"———"———"———"——— TAIL PIPE ⅛ COOL UNTIL SHUT-DOWN.	NO LEAKS – SOME SMOKE FROM EXHAUST TROUSER CUT-OFF WITH L.P. COCK
SALT FLATS	3	POT HOLES ON COURSE 'N' 1 MILE MAX 4' X 2' X 3' DEEP. LOOSE.	
———"———	4	———"———"———	
———"———	5	———"———	VERY GOOD RUN.
———"———	6	BAD OVER FIRST PART OF COURSE. LOOSE SWEEPINGS BLACK LINE	CRASH.

79

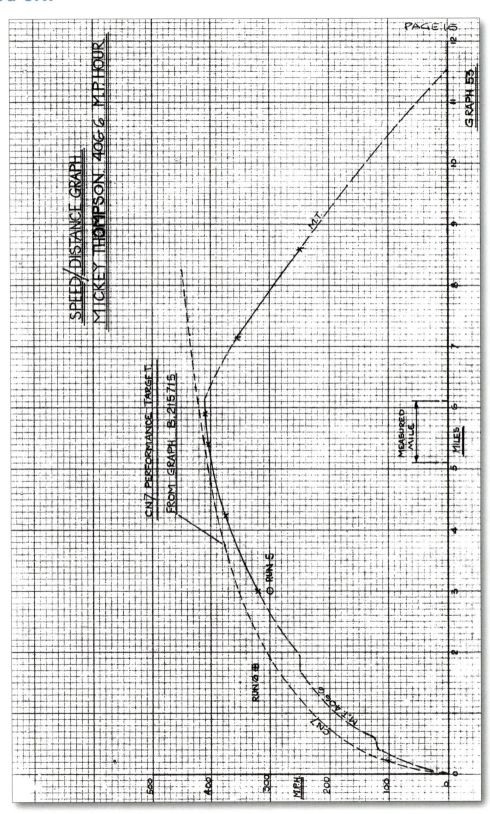

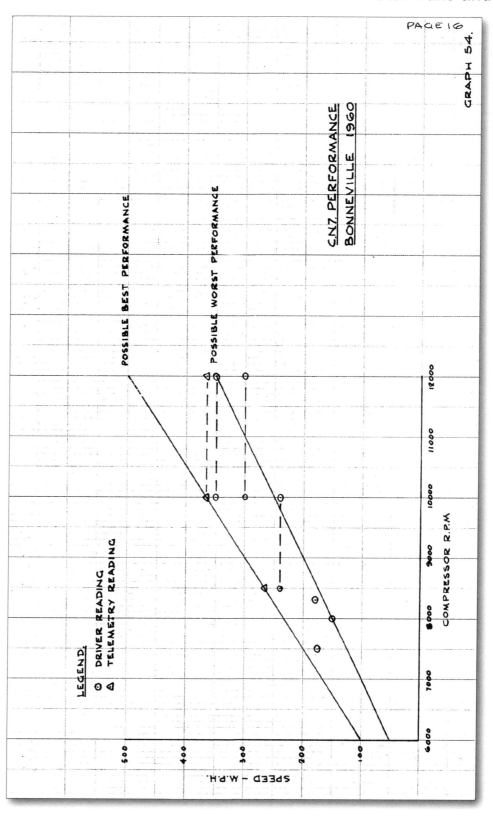

LEGEND:
⊙ DRIVER READING
△ TELEMETRY READING

POSSIBLE BEST PERFORMANCE

POSSIBLE WORST PERFORMANCE

CN7 PERFORMANCE
BONNEVILLE 1960

PAGE 16.

GRAPH 54.

SPEED – M.P.H.

COMPRESSOR R.P.M.

Bluebird CN7

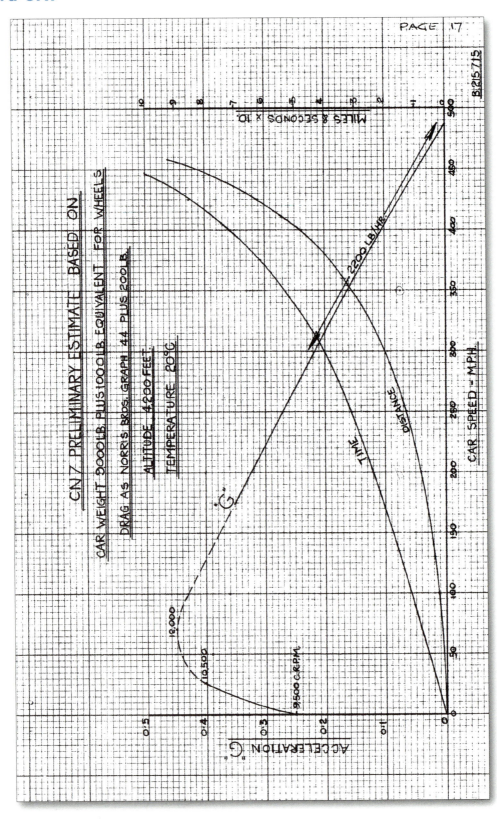

CN7 PRELIMINARY ESTIMATE BASED ON

CAR WEIGHT 3000LB. PLUS 1000LB. EQUIVALENT FOR WHEELS

DRAG AS NORRIS BROS. GRAPH 44. PLUS 200LB.

ALTITUDE 4200 FEET.

TEMPERATURE 20°C.

PAGE 17

B.215.715

MILES & SECONDS x 10.

CAR SPEED — M.P.H.

ACCELERATION "G".

2200 LB./HP.

DISTANCE

TIME

"G"

12,000

10,500

9,500 C.R.P.M.

82

11. C.N.7 Goodwood Trials 18.7.60 to 22.7.60

1. General

JULY The C.N.7 arrived at Goodwood during the night of Sunday, 17th August 1960, for power runs before the press and public and for various static tests and final adjustments to be made before shipment. At approximately 10 a.m. C.N.7 was unloaded from its transporter, a mark being made on each tyre where the wheel centre line cut the ground line, this point being checked as C.N.7 was rolled down the ramps, in order to assess transmission wind up which was found to be negligible.

2. Towed Run 18.7.60

At approximately 3 p.m. C.N.7 was towed around the Goodwood circuit using Land Rovers as tug and anchor vehicles on front and rear towing eyes.

The cavalcade proceeded at about $4\frac{1}{2}$ m.p.h. to a point about a third of the way around the course where it stopped in order that C.N.7's gearboxes could be filled with oil. During the tow, two noises were heard, these being attributed to:-

(i) The brake discs slopping on their locating keys, and

(ii) The engine turbine blades slopping in the turbine disc due to rotation whilst cold.

The tow then proceeded at 10-15 m.p.h., C.N.7 turning all corners with ease, and the final lap speed, excluding the stop for oil, was $11\frac{1}{2}$ m.p.h.

3. D.M.C's comments

Everything was satisfactory, the handling being exceptionally good.

4. Static Engine Runs 1 and 2 20.7.60

The two static engine runs were carried out in the hangar at 6.40 and 6.48 and were respectively of 30 secs. and 1 min. 40 secs. at 5,000 c.r.p.m. Paint was burnt and blistered around the rear end of the exhaust pipe, there being some buckling of the skin at the fore and aft ends of the exhaust opening. This would have to be remedied but was satisfactory for present conditions.

5. Static Engine Runs 3 and 4 21.7.60

These took place on the circuit at 12.59 and 13.48 and were for 6 mins. and 3 mins. respectively. The runs were to give D.M.C. practice in cockpit drill and starting and stopping the engine. Further buckling took place around the exhaust outlets and it was found that servicing panel cover could be easily distorted if hot when removed.

The distortion and overheating were being caused by the differential expansion of the stainless steel shroud and the aluminium structure to which it was riveted, and by the bad fit of the exhaust pipe extension. Action was taken to remedy this before running at Bonneville.

6.   Goodwood Run 1   21.7.60

The run was made with fire and service vehicles in attendance, the speedometer of the fire tender, the closest to C.N.7 reading between 10 m.p.h. and 48 m.p.h. All corners were taken slowly but with ample room to spare, air brakes being operated when the pit area was reached.

7.   Goodwood Runs 2, 3 and 4   22.7.60

All runs were uneventful, the main points of note being that Run 3 was for two circuits (19 mins.) and that Peter Carr had his first drive on run 4.

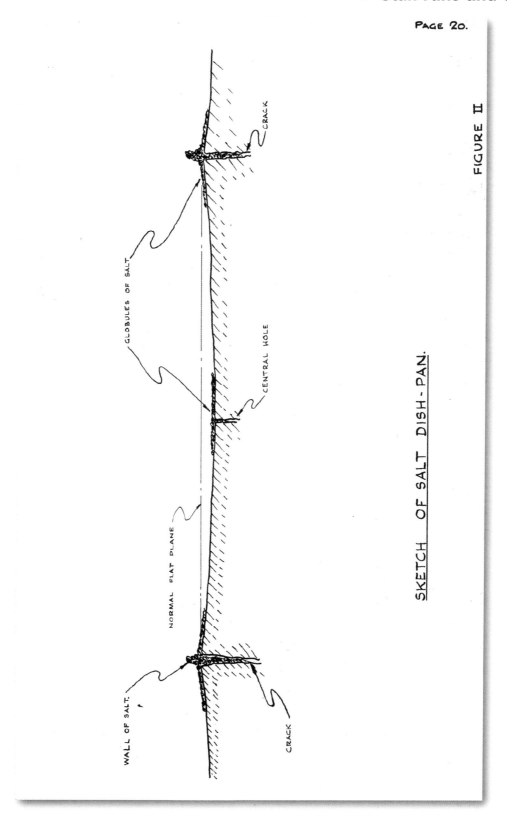

FIGURE II

SKETCH OF SALT DISH-PAN.

CRACK

GLOBULES OF SALT.

CENTRAL HOLE

NORMAL FLAT PLANE

WALL OF SALT.

CRACK

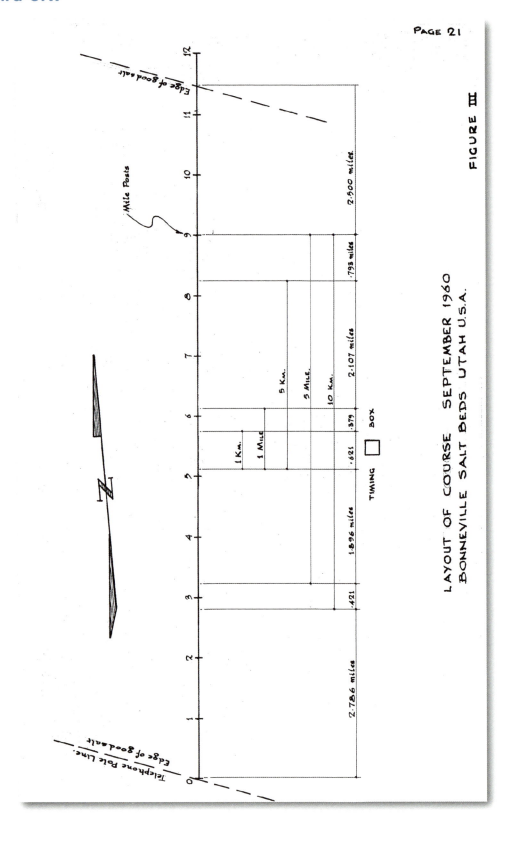

PAGE 21

Edge of good salt

Mile Posts

2.500 miles

.793 miles

5 KM.

5 MILE

10 KM.

2.107 miles

.379

1 KM.

1 MILE

.621

TIMING BOX

1.896 miles

.421

2.786 miles

Telephone Pole Line
Edge of good salt

LAYOUT OF COURSE   SEPTEMBER 1960
BONNEVILLE SALT BEDS UTAH U.S.A.

FIGURE III

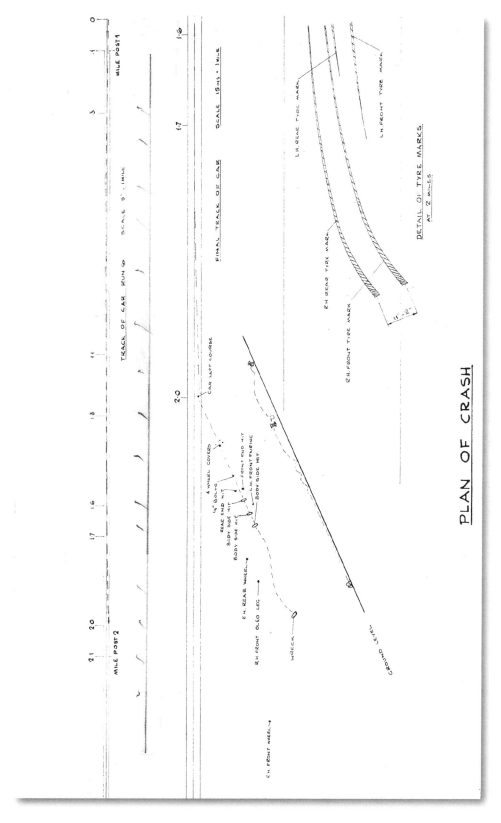

PLAN OF CRASH

Bluebird CN7

12. DAMAGE TO CAR.

(a) <u>Prior to the crash</u>, that is up to the point where the car first rolled on to its side, examination of the tracks left by the car suggest that there was nothing structurally or mechanically wrong. Track measurement remained constant right up to the point of turn off and then the left hand wheel marks tapered uniformly to nothing whilst the right hand wheel marks widened unifromly to a maximum at the point of roll over.

(b) <u>Structure</u>. In general this stood up remarkably well to the pounding it received. The G meter placed above the front axle to record vertical accelerations indicated +8·3 g. and was off the clock at −5.00 g. Wheel covers were blown off, wheel fairings were forced off and local parts of the main beam faces were carried away with the wheel assemblies. The body apart from this appeared to be quite sound except from a twist along its length. The first parts of the car to break appear to have been the steering and track arms, probably due to the very high gyroscopic loads imposed by the wheels during the initial roll over. This allowed the wheels to flap on their king pins and to 'saw' circular lumps out of the main beam faces, thus weakening the structure around the suspension pickups.

(c) <u>Mechanical parts etc</u>. From the short superficial examination so far carried out it is not possible to reach very definite conclusions but in general it is evident that many parts can be salvaged. The engine was still running quite sweetly when the car came to rest after the crash. Transmission had clearly siezed somewhere in the region of the gearboxes. Half shafts had been torn out with suspension assemblies and these had suffered considerably. On removal of the gearbox and plenum chamber covers very little damage could be seen although one gearbox had moved out of line with the engine. The cockpit instrument panel etc. showed very little sign of damage.

13.   COPY OF REPORT TO U.S.A.C.

The general conclusion regarding the crash has been issued
in the form of a statement to U.S.A.C. During the course of
my general investigation I have found nothing to invalidate this
statement which now follows:

"A thorough investigation into the causes of the crash which took
place on the Salt Flats early on Friday morning, the 16th of
September, has reached the following conclusions:

1.   The car went off the track after accellerating for approximately 1 – 3/4 miles from the north and when travelling at a speed
of approximately 350 M.P.H. The following are believed to be the
causes:

    (a)   Crosswind effects.

    (b)   Car running over loose salt and oiled marker line.

    (c)   High output torque from engine.

2.   There is no evidence to show that the car was in any way structurally or mechanically unsound at the time of the crash.

3.   Diagram of area of crash is available showing sequence of break-
up.

4.   The conclusions were agreed by the following:

    P.W. Carr, Operational Manager:

    L.Villa, Chief Engineer:

    D.Badger, Dunlop Rubber Company:

    M.Britton, Chief Construction Engineer:

    K.W.Norris, Co-Chief Designer:

    R.Govier, Bristol-Siddeley Engine Representative:

    C.Noble, Electro-Hydraulics Engineer.

RE—CONSTRUCTION OF CRASH

Distance Travelled	Distance Travelled Off Course	Remarks
		Run started 176 yds. from 0 mile post. R.H. wheels were next to the central marking line.
176 yds.		No sign.
211 yds.		R.H. wheels over line.
616 yds.		L.H. wheels on line.
761 yds.		L.H. wheels over line. Surface of brown loose grained salt with bumps and potholes on L.H. wheel track.
781 yds.		Wheel tracks $66\frac{1}{2}$" apart.
801 yds.		Wheel tracks $66\frac{3}{4}$" apart.
880 yds.		Wheel tracks $66\frac{3}{8}$" apart.
1221 yds.		Wheel tracks $66\frac{1}{4}$" apart.
1496 yds.		Large cracks in salt. Signs of possible ? wheel slip.
1761 yds.		L.H. wheel tracks 4ft. on R.H. side of central marking line.
1 mile 352 yds.		Wheel tracks $66\frac{3}{4}$" apart.
1 mile 520 yds.		L.H. wheels on central marking line. Salt cleared from line, probably by wheels spinning. Wheel tracks $66\frac{3}{8}$" apart.
1 mile 880 yds.		L.H. wheels on central marking line. Line very black, showing wheel spin. Salt getting whiter.
1 mile 1056 yds.		Surface very bad. L.H. wheel tracks over central marking line.
1 mile 1232 yds.		Quadruple tracks start.
1 mile 1409 yds.		Tracks turning to left. Wheel tracks $66\frac{1}{8}$" and $66\frac{1}{2}$" apart. L.H. wheels 20" on L.H. side of line. Tracks continue to move towards left until all are on L.H. side of course. Weight gradually transferring from L.H. wheels to R.H. wheels.
2 miles		L.H. rear wheel loses contact with salt then L.H. front wheel loses contact.
	5 yds.	R.H. front wheel rim digs into salt and pieces of tyre around.
	88 yds.	All four wheel covers blown off as rolls over in the air, presenting its under-surface to the wind.
	163 yds.	Head and shank of three $\frac{1}{4}$" bolts. These appear to be some of the bolts which attached the steering arms to the hub, all of which were sheared due to the high rate of precession imparted to the wheels when the car rolled. Also one fastener found.

Distance Travelled	Distance Travelled Off Course	Remarks
	189 yds.	Tail of car struck salt leaving indentation in salt marked with blue paint, also marks from one rear tyre.
	194 yds.	Front R.H. side of car struck salt. Marks of wheel rim digging in.
	204 yds.	Pieces of tyre rubber scrapped off by inner faces of wheel covers.
	209 yds.	R.H. side of car struck salt, leaving blue marked indentation and wheel rim marks. Also complete R.H. front wheel fairing ripped off
	219 yds.	One $5/16$" washer and one $5/16$" nut found.
	224 yds.	One $5/16$" nut and one balance weight found. The items indicate a wheel rim coming loose.
	234 yds.	L.H. front wheel fairing found.
	239 yds.	Car touched down all along R.H. side leaving indentation marked with blue and wheel rim marks 10ft. 3ins. apart. Also some marks apparently made by the hub nuts.
	244 yds.	Several wheel rim nuts.
	249 yds.	One $\frac{1}{4}$" nut and pieces of honeycomb. Wheel fairing corner bracket.
	254 yds.	The car touched down all along its side leaving a number of wheel rim nuts and fastener pins.
	259 yds.	The car touched down for the final time and began its long slide to rest.
	269 yds.	One tube through bulkhead.
	283 yds.	The R.H. rear wheel fairing together with several pieces of honeycomb and the half shaft gaiter still with its 'Jubilee' clips on. It was probably here or shortly before that the R.H. rear wheel broke free.
	288 yds.	Several wheel nuts and $\frac{1}{4}$" nuts found.
	293 yds.	Some honeycomb, a Uniball ring lying around here.
	323 yds.	Further evidence of wheel breaking away leaving pieces of half shaft seals (both ends), suspension stiffener, small pieces of honeycomb and a 'Jubilee' clip were scattered here. A short distance further on lay a steering arm from the R.H. front wheel.
	333 yds.	The R.H. rear wheel came to rest here complete with suspension leg, steering arm and outer face of main beam with pieces of honeycomb still attached. This piece having been sawn out by the wheel rims.

Distance Travelled	Distance Travelled Off Course	Remarks
	353 yds.	The R.H. front wheel had broken away by now, leaving behind its upper wishbone, the body of its oleo leg, some anchor nuts and pieces of bakelite battery filler.
	453 yds.	The wreck of the car halted here.
	710 yds.	The R.H. front wheel carried on to this point complete with hub and wishbones, outer face of main beam and top of its oleo leg.

15.   Mickey Thompson's Car - Challenger 1 - 12.10.60

15.1 <u>9.10.60</u>   M.T. did 406.6 m.p. South to North through the mile; during the return run one of his main shafts broke at about 2,500 ft. and 170 m.p.h.

15.2 <u>Particulars of Vehicle</u> - From inspection and as a result of discussions with M.T.

    (i)   <u>Layout</u> - 4 Pontiac engines forming 'block' between axles.

                5,000 to 6,000 r.p.m.

                500 + h.p. each.

                Front pair of engines drive front axle.

                Rear pair of engines drive rear axle.

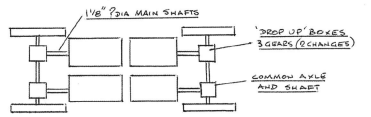

    (ii)   <u>Wheels</u> - are 29½" dia. over tyres and tyres are of flat section.

    (iii)   <u>Suspension</u> - None - i.e. no springing or damping.

    (iv)   <u>Geometry of Steering</u> - 0.090" Toe OUT

                8°   Castor (approx. 2" at ground)

                No camber

                ¼" outboard tyre setting.

    (v)   <u>Ballast and Tyre loading</u> - Trouble was experienced with front wheel slip. As a result 550 lb. approximately ballast was put at the front end for the 406.6 run. Also a 1½" high x approx. 30" wide flow deflector was placed about 40% distance up the sloping nose of the car. On weighing the front right hand wheel had 70 lb. and the rear left hand wheel 20 lb. extra load.

    (vi)   <u>Stopping from high speed</u> -

        (a)   Engine drag down for approximately 2 miles, pumping brakes meantime.

        (b)   Parachute - twin slotted.

        (c)   Mechanical (hydraulic operated) brakes on 100 m.p.h.

    (vii)   <u>Frontal area and elevation</u> - Quoted as being 15½ sq.ft.

Bluebird CN7

Page 29.

Mickey Thompson's Car (contd.)

    (vii) Frontal area and elevation (contd.)

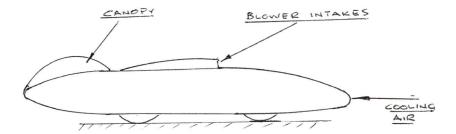

(NOTE: M.T. states that he is already making a new car with
small gas turbine engines).

(He has picture of air pressure distribution for C.N.7 –
taken with permission of K.W.N.)

Reckons to be back in two weeks with car repaired.

DMC and Peter Carr (right) with Micky Thomson. (Peter Carr Collection)

LIST OF PERSONNEL AT SALT FLATS

Peter Carr	Director of Operations	D.M.Campbell
Tommy Wisdom	Operational Adviser	Independent
Norman Buckley	Track Marshall	"
Leo Villa	Chief Mechanic	D.M.Campbell
Maurice Parfit		"
Brian Coppock		"
Phil Villa		"
Ken Ritchie		"
Ken Norris	Designer	Norris Brothers Ltd.
Ray Govier		Bristol-Siddeley Eng.
Allan Potton		Sir W.G.Armstrong-Whitworth
Maurice Britton		Motor Panels
Maurice Bullock		"
Tom Scrimshire		"
Ron Williss		Girling Ltd.
Tom Lawson		"
Maurice Edwards		J.Lucas
Don Badger		Dunlop Ltd
Albert Garland		"
Sid West		"
Jim O'Connor		Dunlop (Buffalo)
John Gullery		"
Andrew Mustard		Dunlop Ltd.
Carl Noble		Electro-Hydraulics
Bob Hudson		Rover (England)
Neville News		" "
Nick Wilks		" (Toronto)
Dick Green		" (San Fransisco)
David Cobham	Film Producer	R.H.R Productions
Leon Bijou	Cameraman	" "
Brian Cooper	P.R.O.	B.P
Robin Kirkby	Assistant Director of Operations	B.P
Ken Babb		Cummins Engine Co.Inc.
Ed Kolenovski	Chief Photographer	Associated Press
Ken Reaks		Smiths

Page 31

List of Personnel at Salt Flats – contd.

Earl Heath	Western Motel & Service Stn.
Colonel Gentry	Air Force Base, Hillfield
Lt.Colonel Smith	"
James R.Brown	"
Howard Green	"
Capt. Weaver	Air Force Base, Wendover
David Wadsworth	"
Richard Turley	University of Utah
Roland Portwood i/c Salt Grading	–
Ed Ramsey	B.P Canada
Amie Juteau	"
Bill Davies	B.P America
Carroll Thompson	"

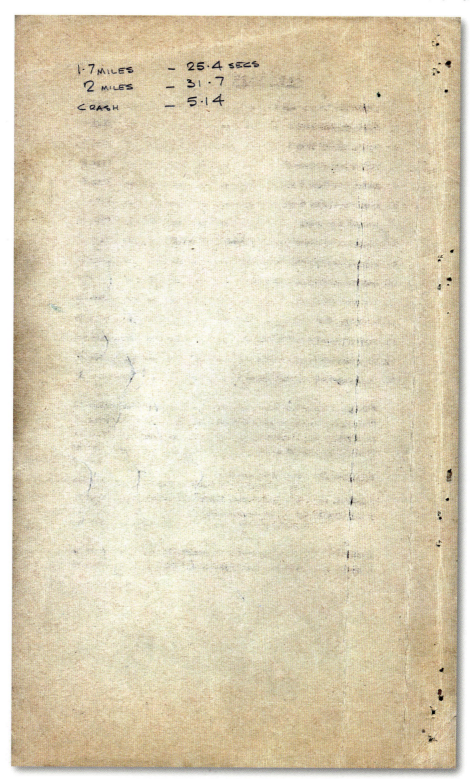

1.7 MILES   — 25.4 SECS
2 MILES   — 31.7
CRASH   — 5.14

End of report.

Artist's impression of salt flats. (BP Archive)

DMC at the controls of the Piper Commanche that was loaned to the team. (BP Archive)

Bonneville Salt Flats from the air, with only the left-hand side of the track cleared. The small black dots to the left are vehicles at base camp. The circular track, part of which is shown, was used by hot-rods.
(Peter Carr Collection)

Working on CN7 in the hangar at Wendover. BP support Land Rovers in the background. (BP Archive)

Left: Loading CN7 onto its trailer at Wendover. The long ramp was necessary due to the small ground clearance of CN7. (BP Archive)

Bottom: Servicing CN7 on turnaround. The shiny cans on top are fans drawing cooling air over the brakes. DMC, Ken Norris and Peter Carr stand at the front discussing the run. (BP Archive)

Now where did I put my helmet? (BP Archive)

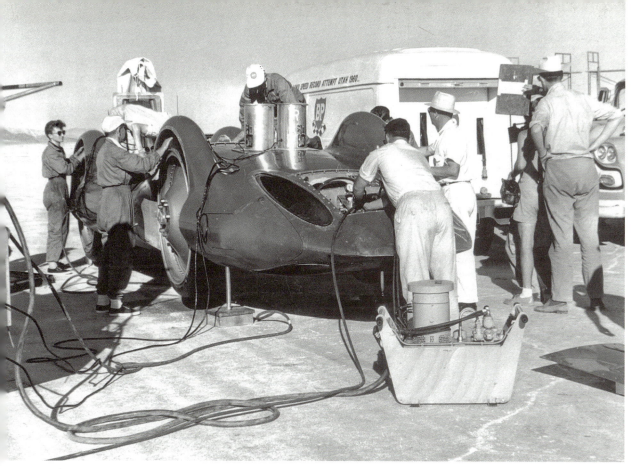

Servicing CN7 on turnaround. BP fuel bowser behind it. (BP Archive)

Whilst others pose, Ken Norris works! (BP Archive)

Left: Tyre marks left by CN7 going sideways at over 300mph!
(BP Archive)

Bottom: Four wheel covers blown off when somersaulting.
(BP Archive)

Below: Wheel, halfshaft and wishbone.
(BP Archive)

Opposite page:

Top: The final slide.
(BP Archive)

Bottom left: Structure cut away by wheel rim.
(BP Archive)

Bottom right: Good driver protection.
(BP Archive)

Bluebird CN7

The 'black oil line' mentioned in the report had been very effectively used for many years, and it did not occur to anyone that it might be hazardous if two wheels, with the very high torque available in CN7, ran on it for even a short distance. A black or dark blue dye is now used.

The decision to change the steering ratio from 25:1 to 100:1 was undoubtedly a bad one. Ken Norris wrote to me saying that it was going to be changed, and I responded by letter on 8th September saying: "If the steering is too sensitive, a reduction in the amount of offset (ie reduced track) of the front wheels should be tried first. It seems rather silly to put the ratio up to 100:1 without trying the lower ratio at reasonable speed. If Reid Railton [the designer of John Cobb's Railton Mobil Special, the current Land Speed Record holder which had a 25:1 ratio, who was living in the US] turns up, it would be good to ask his opinion." By way of explanation to younger readers, telephone calls and telegrams (the nearest equivalent to faxes and texts) were prohibitively expensive, so Air Mail letters taking 2-3 days were the main form of communication. From notes found during my research for this book, there was considerable unease amongst a number of the technicians from support companies because the change was carried through without sufficient discussion. Several even recorded that they did not have confidence in Leo Villa's decisions because they felt that he was DMC's 'yes man,' and expressed an unwillingness to work under his direction. The most vociferous of these was Maurice Britton, who always said what he thought, and I suspect that this was the main contributing reason for his being 'persona non grata' for the later Australian run. Shades of my experience!

The recommendation in 8(a) on page 12 of the report seems rather harsh on the design team when the severity of the crash and the minor damage that DMC received is taken into account. Next day the wreck received a close examination by Ken Norris and the team. It was obvious from the marks on the track that there was nothing structurally or mechanically wrong with the car when it left the track. The structure stood up remarkably well considering the four-ton vehicle travelling at over 300mph had flown more than 200yds (183m), and bounced three times before sliding to a halt. The 'g' meter sited above the front axle recorded +8.3g, and was off the clock at -5g. The wheel covers and a wheel fairing had been blown off when the car rotated sideways travelling through the air and presented its underside to the direction of travel. The massive gyroscopic forces on the 52in (1.32m) diameter wheels, weighing 420lb (190kg) each, rotating at 3000rpm and being precessed at a very high rate, broke the steering and track arms, freeing the wheels

to slam about on their king pins and allow the wheel rims to cut through the structure. (To get an idea of the forces involved, readers could try holding a bicycle wheel by its axle, spinning it, and then trying to turn it quickly through 90 degrees.) Despite this, the structure remained essentially in one piece, to the extent that there was no damage in the cockpit area and it took close examination to detect a slight twist along the length of the car. All the wheel-related parts were damaged beyond repair, but the engine and gearboxes appeared re-useable, as did most of the auxiliary components.

One modification which was made, but not listed in the report, was to replace the 'Perspex' bubble canopy with one made of 0.75in (1.9cm) thick reinforced glass fibre. This was mainly to improve driver vision by reducing

BP advertisement for MG class record. (BP Archive)

glare in the cockpit, but also to provide greater driver protection in the event of another accident.

When delving into the archives at the Science Museum, I found a letter from Basil Markham, Bristol-Siddely's chief designer, sent to Ken Norris after the crash, which stated: "The power doubles between 10,500 and 12,000crpm." This would be a massive surge of over 2000hp, which, due to the fluid drive nature of the gas turbine, would easily catch the driver unaware, and would corroborate Don Badger's comment. This power surge had not been pointed out by Bristol-Siddeley before!

In the aftermath of the crash there was much press speculation as to whether Stirling Moss should have driven the car. He had been breaking 1250cc and 1500cc Class Records for MG, but I am not alone in believing that, as DMC found, CN7 – with its very different power delivery to that of piston engines – required other skills, more akin to those of fighter pilots. Also, the Campbell name is associated with ultimate speed records and the 'Bluebird' name. To illustrate this, I offer a story told to me by Sid Enever, the chief designer for MG. In 1956 MG engaged Moss to drive its 1500cc record attempt car. The team was on site, conditions were ideal for about a week before Moss was due to arrive, and in trial runs Sid broke the record by a substantial margin. The day before Moss arrived it rained heavily and the surface did not fully dry out before he was due to leave. Moss managed to break the record despite the adverse conditions, but at about 20mph (32kph) slower than Sid's recorded trial times. The publicity used Moss' speed!

The accompanying graph shows the speed achieved by Mickey Thompson on his single 406mph (653kph) run, and the projected speed for CN7/60 with the 4000hp engine. When the car crashed, its ultimate speed had been recorded as 330mph (531kph), and for some unknown reason that figure was used to project its ultimate record potential as about 410mph (660kph), and this was without the extra aerodynamic drag of the tail fin added to CN7/62.

However, I now realise that after 0.3 miles (0.48km) of acceleration the car had drifted across the central marker line onto the un-swept side of the course. Maximum traction would not have been available over the loose salt, and the car carried on for about a mile on those conditions before getting its left-hand wheels onto the central oil marker line. This caused the wheels to spin, reducing acceleration even more. As the graph shows, even with a conservative allowance for the impaired acceleration, the potential of CN7/62 with its greater engine power would have been much higher. This is confirmed by the graph on page 116.

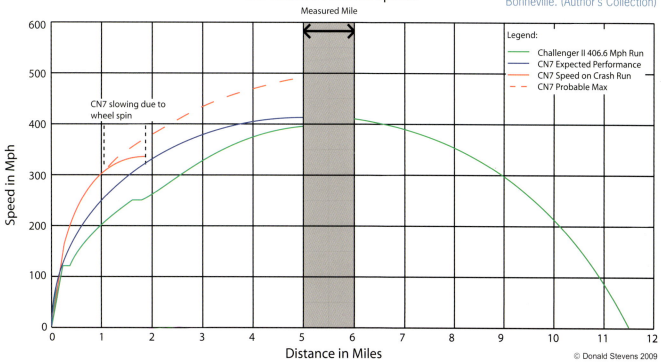

CN7 Actual & Potential Speeds

Speed distance graph from Bonneville. (Author's Collection)

© Donald Stevens 2009

DMC at a post-crash press conference, with Peter Carr's crash helmet which helped save his life. (BP Archive)

A never used but all too prophetic advertisement prepared for BP. (BP Archive)

Rebuild and Australia

On its return to the UK the car was sent direct to Motor Panels for rebuilding, as Sir Alfred had said that if Donald was prepared to drive it again, he would rebuild it. After a very thorough examination of the wreck by Ken and Lew when it was at Motor Panels, it was decided that although the auxiliary and transverse beams looked reusable, the whole of the structure should be rebuilt because it was not possible to asses whether any of the bonding had de-laminated. The new main beams were built with larger, forged attachment points for the suspension arms, and a solid connection from top to bottom for the pneumatic strut. About 80 per cent of the mechanical parts were reusable, but the engine and gearboxes were returned to their constructors for examination. The engine was stripped and rebuilt to a higher specification giving an additional 150hp.

An illustration of how amazingly strong the wheels were comes in a letter dated 30th December 1960, from GE Adams of Dunlop Road Wheel Division to Norris Brothers, which states " ... received 16 Land Speed Record wheels for inspection purposes. So far we have established that the four wheels used on the final run are *virtually* scrap." They were re-designed for the rebuilt car with a weight saving of 30lb (13.61kg) per wheel. Also around that time, Ransome and Marles, who had made all of the ball and roller bearings, reported that its " ...

test department had inspected the hubs and found no damage, but new bearings will be made."

Maurice Britton took over my role as project co-ordinator for CN7/62, as the rebuilt car was to be designated, as it would save on costs, and by now he had an excellent grasp of the car's design. There was probably some considerable influence from Leo that I should not be included due to our falling out over the engine installation. Interestingly, whilst researching this book, I found three reports from support company members of the team which indicated that they were not happy to work under his control in future! Peter Carr, who had been reserve driver and project manager at Bonneville, left the team on its return to the UK to join the BP Sales Promotion Team.

Most of the recommendations listed by the team after the crash were there to reduce the damage should another 'take off' happen – a somewhat unlikely event! Most were easily accommodated, but the aerodynamic fin created most discussion. The stability of the car was perfectly adequate without such an addition, providing the tyres did not lose their adhesion, something that could be avoided with experience, and which was reduced by the use of a blue dye marker line in Australia. The fin's only use would be to keep the car from slewing *if airborne*, but it added a considerable amount of drag, a most undesirable feature. It did however enable the

Bluebird CN7

installation of a camera housing which provided some very interesting film and some useful data, and, from a publicity point of view, showed that modifications had been made.

One modification, about which very little has been recorded, was a throttle control system designed by Gordon Dale-Smith, who had been responsible for the telemetry system in CN7/60. The system was designed to control the rate at which the throttle could be opened by incremental steps with an adjustable time delay incorporated between each step, thereby keeping the initial acceleration under control. A braking parachute was installed, without the gyroscopic trip system, as that was considered a possible danger should it malfunction.

The last item concerning driver protection raised some eyebrows back in the more detached atmosphere of the design office. Remember, the car had flown for 350 yards (274m), somersaulted and bounced three times, had a major part of its structure cut away, before sliding another 400 yards (360m). After all of this, DMC had, in his own words: "Only minor concussion and a small crack in his skull," plus some minor bruising, and walked away from the wreck. It also took an experienced eye, looking along the centre section from the front, to see the distortion in the car's body. However, where possible, padding was added to prevent limbs knocking against hard edges.

Because of the large number of senior businessmen that I had met during my time as project co-ordinator for

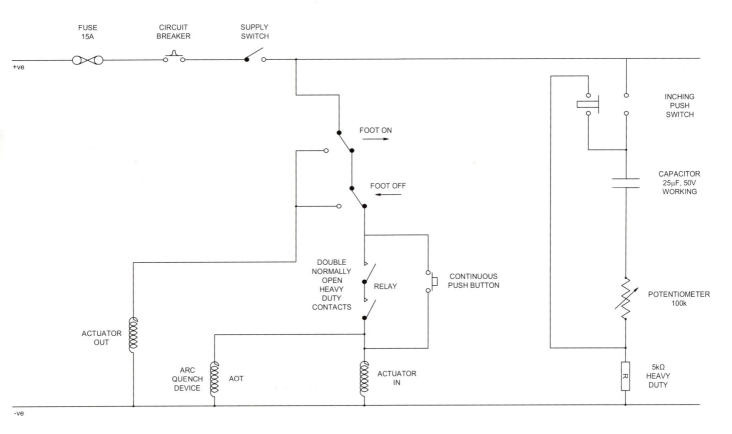

Throttle control circuit. (Author's Collection)

Steering wheel showing stepping control buttons and R/T buttons on steering wheel. (Varndell Collection)

The rebuilt car.
(National Motor
Museum)

Bluebird CN7

CN7/60, the company asked me to take over new business development from Ken and Lew. I also undertook the many lectures on the design of the car at technical institutions around the country, although Ken and Lew did the prestigious ones at 'headquarters' in London.

Early in this book I mention that the reason why Norris Brothers Ltd was best suited to the task of designing the Campbell-Norris 7 would become apparent during the course of the book, and I have told of our experience with one record breaking designer. When assigned the task of lecturer I was told that the PR company, McFarlane-Watson, employed to handle Norris Brothers' publicity, was organising all requests. I was duly told the date of my first one and asked to collect Mr McFarlane from McFarlane-Watson's Kensington office at 4pm. For some reason, I had not asked the affiliation of the group to which I was to give the lecture, nor its location. McFarlane told me to head up the then vestigial M1, and it was not until we were driving up it that I asked where we were headed. Mild apprehension ensued when I learned that the destination was Coventry, the centre of UK car production, and outright panic when I was told that my first lecture was to members of the Institution of Mechanical Engineers (Automotive Division). The lecture went well and at the end was opened up to questions. Immediately the question arose: "What right does Norris Brothers have to design such a vehicle when there was all the experience in Coventry?" Occasionally inspiration comes

Lecture poster. (Author's Collection)

to one's rescue in tight corners, and I remembered the difficulty we had had in finding information on the effects of wheel caster and camber. I asked: "How many chief or senior designers are here?" About six hands went up, so I tore some sheets out of my note pad and asked them each to write down their thoughts on the subject. The replies were brought to me after many less hostile questions, and each one was different! I was able to say that our unbiased approach was best when exploring uncharted territory.

It was a great learning experience facing knowledgeable engineering audiences, even after hearing such comments as: "Eee bah goom ees yung in't ee" (Wow! He's young isn't he?), when my back was turned to one group of venerable engineers in the north of England; I was by then the great age of 24! Or, part way into a lecture to over 300 engineers, hundreds of miles from home, seeing my elder brother's best friend grinning at me from the second row of the audience!

Because Goodwood had a prior booking, trials of the rebuilt car took place initially at RAF Tangmere on the Sussex coast nearby, and then finished at Goodwood. No problems were experienced and the car was deemed ready to make its next attempt at the record.

The problem then arose of where that next attempt would take place. The Utah course was only suitable for record attempts between late July and late September due to its winter flooding, and over the years a progressively shorter run was available, down to 9.5 miles (15km) by 1963. This was considered much too short for a 400+mph (579+kph) attempt, but, based on the acceleration achieved in Australia, would have been adequate and would have provided a much

more accommodating site. British Petroleum searched worldwide for other suitable sites, and Australia proved the most attractive. Not only were there several very large salt lakes, but the Australian Government offered military help to prepare the surface, and State Governments were keen to help financially because they saw the tourism value.

Whilst the car was being rebuilt all of the major suppliers (BP, Rubery Owen, Dunlop, Bristol-Siddeley and Lucas/Girling) found that they were in agreement that any future runs should be controlled by a team manager appointed by them. A contract was drawn up and put to DMC, who rejected the idea outright. He won the day by arguing that if he was killed on a run under the control of their appointee, then his successors could sue them for negligence and the adverse publicity would be enormous. He conceded one point, that Jim Philips, Managing Director of Motor Panels, should visit both Bonneville and Australia to provide an opinion on which was the most suitable site. Jim came down in favour of Lake Eyre in Australia.

Both Bluebird CN7 and K7 were shipped out with the express purpose of DMC becoming the first man to break both land and water speed records in one year; a feat never previously achieved, nor beaten since. Lake Eyre, 400 miles (644km) north of Adelaide in South Australia was chosen for the attempt on the Land Speed Record. Many thousands of years ago it had been a vast inland lake, but now received water on very rare occasions, sometimes as long as 15 years between inundations, and had several places where a course of 12-15 miles (19-24km) could be established. The Australian Army constructed a causeway across the outer, muddy edges

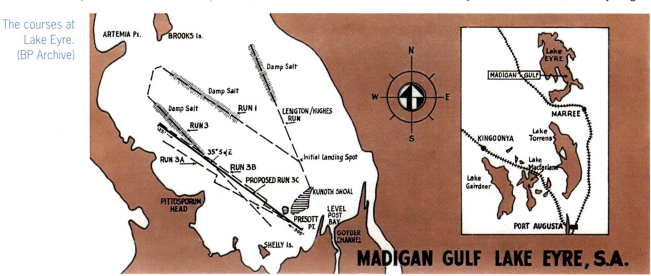

The courses at Lake Eyre. (BP Archive)

The team at Muloorina on the first visit. (BP Archive)

Course preparation – marking the course centre-line. (Rubery Owen Archive)

Ken Norris demonstrating that conditions are more suitable for a water speed record. (Rubery Owen Archive)

of the lake, and improved the approach road over a distance of 30 miles. Preparation of the track needed salt 'islands' to be graded flat over an area 220ft (67m) wide and 15 miles long. Everything was ready by March 15th, but on the 16th intense rain started and continued for a week, with more than even a 'wet' year's normal rainfall. Three weeks later the course was sufficiently dry for preliminary runs to start. The rain started again and continued spasmodically over the next three weeks, causing major flooding and the abandonment of the attempt. The next run was scheduled for 25th April but again heavy rain intervened. A new course about one mile to the east of the other course, with fewer 'salt islands' was found and prepared, and from May 1st to 13th a number of increasingly fast trial runs were made reaching a maximum of 260mph (418.4kph) on only 25 per cent power. Two massive freak storms followed on consecutive days necessitating abandonment of any further attempts for some time. The car was removed from the flats and taken to base camp for a total clean up, rust inhibition and brake pad change, which took a further three weeks. The team came home to await better conditions the following year, whilst the car and boat were stored in Adelaide. BP began to question its involvement, especially when it learned that Ampol, the big Australian oil company was having talks with DMC, and in March 1964 BP withdrew from the project leaving the path clear for Ampol.

Leo and 'Morri' Parfitt returned in February 1964 to check over and prepare both vehicles for a further attempt in May. However, similar problems continued with more rain, different courses, cross winds and poor salt conditions. Even when salt conditions were good, they deteriorated rapidly with increased air temperature, because the heat pulled water toward the surface. Overnight the water table would be 5 inches (13cm) below the surface, but by midday it would rise to only 1 inch (2.5cm) below, making the surface much weaker. These delays lead to some people, including Stirling Moss, to voice their opinion that DMC was not up to the task and a Grand Prix driver would be more appropriate. Of course the 'News Hounds' made great play of that but they were not out there experiencing the worst weather conditions ever known in the area. Also, a Grand Prix driver has much greater practice learning his car and the conditions of the circuit. Courage is one of the greatest requirements for world speed record breaking, and DMC had plenty of that. Due to the continuing poor weather conditions several courses had to be prepared when a chosen one deteriorated. This was no mean task as they had to be at least 11 miles (17.7km) long and 220ft (67m) wide. Many tons of salt islands had to be removed by the Australian Army and its helpers. However, on July 17th DMC eventually broke the Land Speed Record at 403.10mph (648.73kph) with a peak of 440mph (708kph) recorded by the on-board instrumentation. This speed, despite the tyres gouging out grooves in the salt, in places 4 inches deep and 8 inches wide (10cm x 20cm), for miles, together with the acceleration shown at Bonneville confirmed that the Campbell-Norris 7 was undoubtedly capable of considerably more than it's 450mph (724kph) design speed. It is a great pity that the *Guinness Book of Records*

Ken and DMC checking the ruts. (Rubery Owen Archive)

does not have a classification for the fastest plough on earth – CN7 would still hold it! One previously unrecorded fact that came to light recently was that on June 4th DMC allowed Lex Davidson, the Australian grand prix driver, to take Bluebird for a 'spin' over a distance of about 3 miles (4.8km) at speeds of 80-100mph (129-161kph), a rare occurrence as DMC was very protective of his 'baby' – or was it 'mistress'?

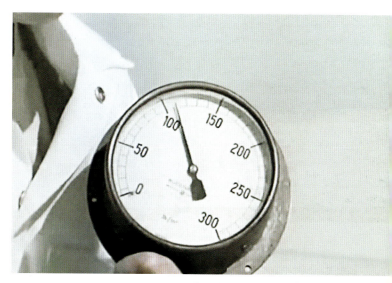

Top left: Changing wheels. (Rubery Owen Archive)

Above: What was left of a tyre after the record run.
(Rubery Owen Archive)

Top right: But no loss of pressure – 120psi.
(Rubery Owen Archive)

Middle right: Driver's eye view. (Rubery Owen Archive)

Bottom right: Braking parachute deployed.
(Rubery Owen Archive)

Opposite: Refuelling from the BP bowser. (BP Archive)

Bluebird CN7

The water speed record was broken at 276.33mph (444.71kph) on Lake Dumbleyung at the 'eleventh hour' in December, making DMC the only man so far, and probably forever, to achieve 'the double' in one year.

The actual record achieved was nowhere near the potential of the car, which, with the rebuilt engine capable of delivering 4200hp should have been over 500mph (804kph). Earlier on in this book, we saw from the recordings of the crash run at Bonneville how the speed potential of CN7/60 was over 500mph. This is confirmed by analysis of some recordings made when the record was broken at 403mph (648kph) by CN7/62. The accompanying graph shows a full record of the South-North run, and a partial record of the return run. The recording of the out run is most interesting as it shows the car abruptly reducing its acceleration long before the measured mile and then rapidly accelerating again just before entering the mile. With both DMC and Ken Norris now deceased we have to think that DMC was so engrossed in controlling the car that he omitted to press the power limiting override switch that had been fitted to the steering wheel (see page 108 and 109), and took about 25 seconds to realise his omission. The waver in the early part of the 'flat' area was probably due to extra drag from the tyres carving the deep ruts through the salt surface. If we take the speed curve A1 to A2 and transpose it across to the extended initial acceleration line to B1 and B2; then take it further at a probable, but not exaggerated, speed increase we reach a potential of about 520mph (837kph). A slightly higher speed is indicated by doing a similar extrapolation of the return run recording, so a potential maximum record speed of 550mph (885kph) seems reasonable. The sharp drop off at 440mph (708kph) on both runs probably shows that a speed limit had been programmed in. From this and the previous deductions it is perfectly feasible to claim that CN7 is the still the fastest wheel-driven car ever built, but does not have the official timed record to prove it. Unfortunately, due to its age and unknown condition of the adhesives in the structure, that will not happen now. Many people, including myself, believe that a car has to be driven through its wheels. CN7/62 even drove under its own power on public roads in Melbourne! This in no way detracts from the amazing efforts and bravery of those drivers, or should it be pilots, such as the writer of the Foreword to this book, who blast their way to mind-blowing speeds, but their vehicles are not driven through the wheels.

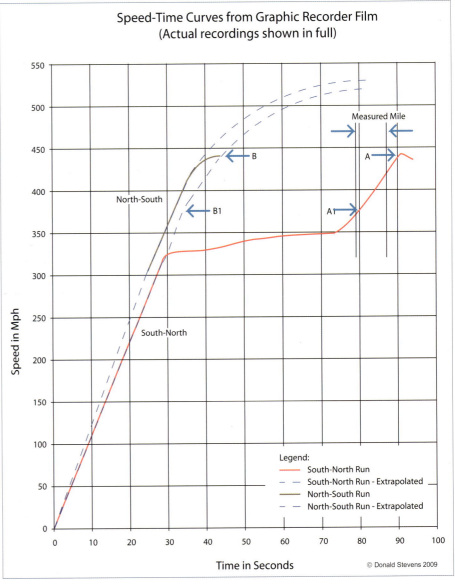

Speed distance graph from record runs. (Author's Collection)

116

Another example of the advanced thinking that came from Norris Brothers was as a result of our designing CN7. In 1962, Sir Alfred Owen was keen to keep BRM at the forefront of Grand Prix racing, and asked us to look at the V8 car that it was using to see if we could suggest any improvements. A number of mainly aerodynamic suggestions were made, including the suggestion that transverse 'wings' should be used at the rear to improve downforce on the tyres at speed. We received a response from Raymond Mays (later Sir Raymond Mays) who headed the technical side of BRM, saying that in no way could such a device be used on a formula one car! It was six years later, in 1968, that manufacturers such as Lotus started experimenting with the idea.

The BRM alongside CN7. (Rubery Owen Archive)

Unlucky Friday the 13th

A rather macabre episode happened in the early evening of Friday 13th January 1961. Being Friday, most people left the office at 5pm, and, as I had a date with my future wife that evening, I was amongst them. Norris Brothers' offices backed on to an unlit public car park, and I went to my car with Gordon Dale-Smith and a group of office girls. Gordon travelled to work from Brighton and used a company mini-bus to transport staff from outlying villages on his way to and from work. It was a very dark evening and my car was parked next to the mini-bus, so Gordon suggested that I reversed out first as it would take a while for his passengers to embark. I moved between the two vehicles to open my car door, only to stumble over what seemed like a pile of rags. A few expletives flowed about idiots dumping rubbish, and Gordon went to the far side of the mini-bus to get a torch. Imagine my horror on shining the torch between the vehicles to see that the 'pile of rags' had a body inside them.

Tony Halliday, one of the draughtsmen who also used the bus, took the girls back to the office, and Gordon ran to the police station which, fortunately, was only about 100 yards away. Years later Gordon told me that when he announced the problem the desk officer shouted along the corridor: "Hey Sarge, a chap here says there's a dead body in the cinema car park." The reply came back: "Oh bugger, I've just made the tea!" On arrival the police confirmed that there was no life in the body and sealed off the area, asking Gordon and I to go to the police station, and sending an officer to interview Tony and the girls. Other staff and the directors organised transport home for them. By this time the police had established that a single stab from a long, sharp, one inch blade had caused the damage. The local police contacted Sussex headquarters, which in turn sent for Scotland Yard murder specialists! Gordon and I were questioned extensively but not allowed to leave the police station. The fact that a policeman sat with us even when questioning was over, and they would not allow us to telephone anyone did not alarm us unduly. It was not until midnight when they released us that we were informed that, as we had found the body, we were chief suspects until someone else was 'in the frame!' We did eventually manage to get them to telephone our homes and my girlfriend, but they would not tell them anything other than that we were 'helping them with enquiries' into an incident. My car was impounded as part of the murder scene so the police put a squad car at my disposal, giving me the opportunity to go to my girlfriend's house and give a limited explanation of the reason for my absence. Having been released at midnight, it was 1am before I managed to slide into bed, only to be woken at 2am by loud knocking on the front door of the house. It was a reporter from one of the national dailies wanting my story. He was sent away with a few choice words in his ear! The police denied all possibility of my address being leaked, of course, but I fail to see how it could have been anyone else.

Fortunately, the culprit was apprehended the next day and the story came out that the victim had been having an affair with a butcher's wife, and butchers' knives are very sharp! The story hit the headlines all over the UK, including all of the major dailies.

Daily Mirror

2½d. Saturday, January 14, 1961 No. 17,753

MURDER IN A CAR PARK— FATHER STABBED

A FATHER of three was stabbed to death in a car park yesterday evening as filmgoers filed into a brightly-lit cinema a few yards away.

An office worker stumbled on the body of fifty - three - year - old William Charles Wood, lying face upwards between a van and a car in the rain-drenched car

William Charles Wood

park of the Orion cinema at Burgess Hill, Sussex.

The time was 5.35 p.m. Police believe that Mr. Wood, a factory worker, died only minutes before.

He had paid with his life for doing a workmate a good turn.

For when he finished work at an engineering factory at 5 p.m., Bill Wood did not go straight home to The Quadrant, at the nearby village of Hassocks.

Friend's Car

He drove a friend to the cinema car park—using the friend's car—because the friend is a learner driver, and could not drive on his own.

At 5.10 he parked the car, handed the keys to his friend and walked off.

Twenty-five minutes later Mr. Donald Stevens, 25, of America-lane, Hayward's Heath, Sussex, went to collect his car, and found Mr. Wood's body.

Police covered the spot with tarpaulin and set up arc lights in the car park. Car owners were not allowed to move their vehicles.

Later, as Scotland Yard men were on their way to the scene, a senior Sussex detective said that Mr. Wood had been paid last evening and robbery could not be ruled out.

Mr. Wood lived with his wife and three children Bill, 17, an apprentice printer, Ann, 19, an insurance clerk and Janet, 22, a bank clerk.

NORRIS BROTHERS LIMITED

From "The Daily Mirror",   14th January, 1961

Daily Mirror

2½d. Saturday, January 14, 1961 No. 17,753

STAB DEATH IN CAR PARK

A FATHER of three was stabbed to death in a car park last night as filmgoers filed into a brightly-lit cinema a few yards away.

12 EVENING ARGUS, 14/1/61

Death park guard

Police stand guard over the Bur[ ] which the body of 53-year-old Mr [ ]

BLUEBIRD MAN FINDS MURDER

Express Staff Reporter

A MAN was found stabbed to death last night in a car park at Burgess Hill, Sussex. Scotland Yard was called in. Mr Donald Stevens, a young engineer working at the Norris Brothers' plant on Donald Campbell's speed car Bluebird, found the man lying between a car and a small bus which five girls were boarding.

The girls ran back into the Norris works. The bus driver gave the alarm at the police station nearby.

The murdered man was identified as William Charles Wood, aged 53, who lived in a new bungalow in the Quadrant at Hassocks, a village on the London-Brighton railway line three miles from Burgess Hill.

QUIZZED

In mist and rain, police sealed the car park. A tarpaulin went up and lamps were installed for doctors to work.

Detective Superintendent Laurie Taylor, of East Sussex C.I.D., took over. Scotland Yard sent Detective Superintendent James Davies. Inquiries spread over the downs to Brighton and along the Sussex coast.

Drivers who went to collect their cars at the park were questioned by police—and asked to leave the cars there for inspection in daylight today.

Mr Wood's 17-year-old son Billy, in short white macintosh was driven from Hassocks to identify him.

What could have been

I n 1963, I was tempted away from Norris Brothers to become marketing advisor to an overseas government in its London Embassy. This chapter, therefore, has been compiled from reports and information held in Ken Norris' archive. I had stayed in sporadic contact with Ken, and on one occasion late in 2005, he asked me to go to the National Motor Museum at Beaulieu to meet Mike Varndell and his team – Paul Hannaford, a surveyor from Somerset, and Nick Chapman, a computer consultant from Birmingham – who were sorting out all of Ken's information which had become jumbled up during several location moves, and had been rescued from a transport container. The National Motor Museum had kindly offered a room in which the data on a number of Norris Brothers projects could be sorted and stored.

All of the original drawings and calculations for K7, CN7/60 and CN7/62 had been deposited by Ken with the Science Museum and, at the time of writing, are held in a very disorganised state in its archive at the old RAF bomber repair facility at Wroughton near Swindon, Wiltshire.

Ken, by then a sick man, was confined to a wheelchair, having had two serious accidents – one with a powered leaf sweeper which overturned on him and broke a number of bones in his lower body, and one in a very spectacular car crash that he was more than fortunate to survive. He told me that he was writing a book on Norris Brothers Ltd, with the help of Mike and his wife, Bernice, and wanted my input, " ... because you played an important part in the early days." I suspect he realised that his health was failing and that I could provide some continuity.

Ken died in October 2006, ten days after my last meeting with him when it had been agreed that I should work with Mike Varndell to continue the writing of his book on Norris Brothers Ltd; a somewhat monumental task, because of all of the ground-breaking developments that stemmed from the company, that will follow this one.

When CN7/60 was at Bonneville Ken realised that DMC would want a faster vehicle to compete with the pure thrust jets of the Americans, and his mind started to examine the possibilities. Interestingly, his first concept was a most unusual design which was intended as a contender for *both* land and water speed records! It would be a four-pointer on water, and then metal wheels would be attached behind the planing shoes for land work. It was proposed to use two Bristol-Siddeley 'Orpheus' jet engines, each with over 5400lb of thrust, giving design speeds of 580mph on land and 400 knots on water. I have redrawn the accompanying scheme drawings from a very crumpled original produced by Fred Wooding in November 1963. Some wind tunnel tests were done, but Ken must have quickly realised that such a vehicle, although plausible, would not have

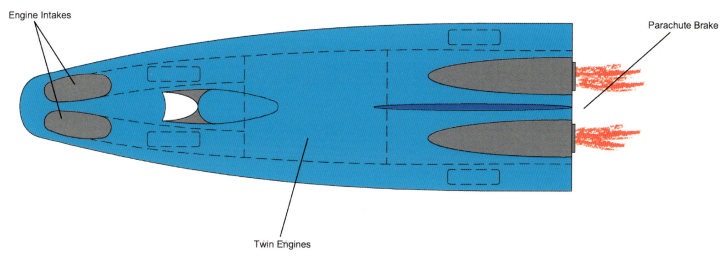

Engine Intakes

Parachute Brake

Twin Engines

OTHER FEATURES:
Mach 0.8 approx
Stressing Case 27g Vertical
Air Ejection Under Hull For Water Separation
Steering - Aerodynamic/Wheel/Planes
Aerodynamically Stable In Pitch And Roll

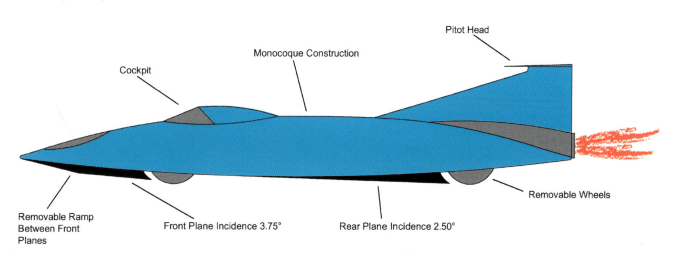

Pitot Head

Monocoque Construction

Cockpit

Removable Wheels

Removable Ramp
Between Front
Planes

Front Plane Incidence 3.75°

Rear Plane Incidence 2.50°

Ken Norris' scheme for a dual purpose record breaker.
(Author's Collection)

© Donald Stevens 2009

had a sufficiently high speed potential on land, and both BP and Dunlop had decided not to back the project, so it was not developed.

After CN7/62 broke the record in Australia in 1964, DMC began talking of a new 'Bluebird' that would become known as CN8. For the new design, Ken had bypassed jet engines, realising that the power/weight ratio provided by rockets would result in a much smaller and lighter vehicle. By this time rocket power had developed to such a stage that it was comparatively safe, and Ken decided that two Bristol-Siddeley BS 605 engines, which had been developed for assisting aircraft take-off, would be ideal. Two engines would be required so that one could be used for low speed trial runs, thus providing for a greater degree of control because rockets do not have a throttle. Each engine produced 7700lb (3493kg) of thrust, an equivalent of 22,610 horsepower!

Bluebird CN7

Unfortunately, most of the people involved with the design of this vehicle have either died or cannot be traced, so the information has been gleaned from two undated reports. The first, by Clive Fletcher, a pupil of Professor John Stollery, then of Imperial College, London, is in a Norris Brothers' report cover and was completed in late 1965. The second was completed some years later, and appears to be a draft of a thesis by GK Dawson of Woolwich Polytechnic, a copy of which Ken passed on to me.

The small size of the rocket motors enabled a design with a very low cross-sectional area, and Ken realised that the main problem would be directional stability. Essentially, the vehicle had to go in a straight line in the direction

that it was pointed when the rockets fired, steering being limited to low speeds only. A dart-like configuration was, therefore, obvious, with the stability in yaw of paramount importance. The other major considerations were to minimise the effect of the sonic wave on the underside of the vehicle, and keeping apart the two highly volatile liquids that, when mixed, provided the fuel for the rocket; especially in the event of an accident. As always, Ken's solution was both simple and practical. The main chassis would be a flat box structure, with internal ribbing, made of ³⁄₁₆in (4.76mm) thick steel that would also provide the frame on which the bodyshell fixed. The engines would be mounted above and below this, with the two highly volatile propellants separated in the same way.

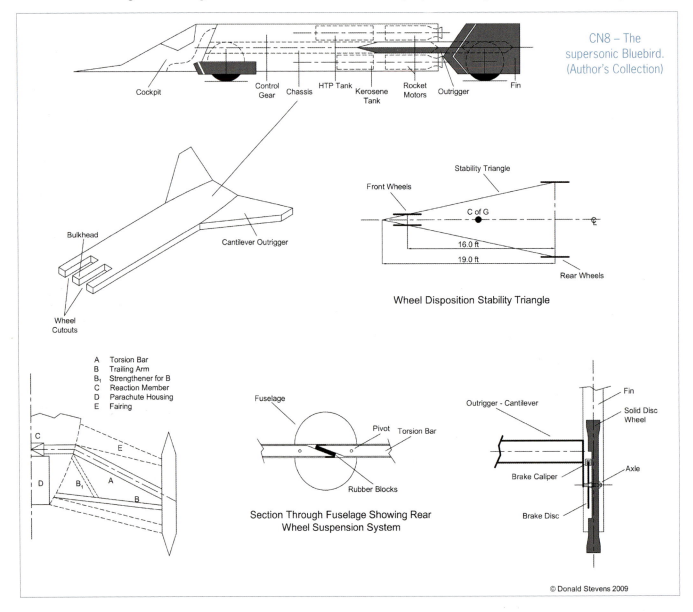

CN8 – The supersonic Bluebird. (Author's Collection)

© Donald Stevens 2009

What could have been

Total weight (calculated)..........3605lb............(1635kg)
Frontal area ....11ft³ ....(1.02m²)
Wheels.....................................2ft 6in dia
x 4in wide ...(76x10cm)

The wheels were to be machined from a single billet of aluminium so there would be no tyres and, therefore, no danger of blow-outs or stripping of rubber. It's safe to assume, then, that Dunlop wouldn't have been a sponsor! The outer surfaces would probably have a 'knurled' finish to provide greater grip. Various suspension systems were examined and most were rejected due to bulk or development needs. The suggested final layout for the rear was that the whole of the outrigger would be used as a cantilever, with loads being taken by rubber blocks, as shown in the drawing (the rubber block in the middle being bonded to both cantilevers, and those above and below acting as bump stops). It was expected that this system would enable a thinner outrigger section. With only +/-½in movement at the wheels being necessary, and a 3:1 lever arm ratio, the movement at the rubber block would be only 0.167in (0.42cm). The front suspension would have been of similar type, but no work was done on the detail.

Aerodynamics would obviously be a very critical aspect of this design, and those of the outriggers of great importance, since they would affect lift (positive or negative) more than any other part of the body. From

Fletcher's report thoroughly examined performance and stability, and showed that a speed of 852mph (1371kph) would be reached in 2.5 miles (4km), but with existing parachute and brake technology it would take a further 9 miles (14.5km) to bring it to a halt! With the measured mile between miles 2-3 on the outward run, it would, therefore, require 16 miles of hard surface to operate. In fact, a greater distance would be required for safety reasons. The rear wheels would be on outriggers, housed in fins which would also provide lateral stability, and the pair of front wheels would be close together behind the driver (remember that four wheels were necessary for the car record). That was in 1963/4, and it was not until 1999 that Thrust SSC reached 763mph (1228kph).

Main dimensions were as follows:

Overall length ....27ft 8in.............(8.43m)
Overall width.............................8ft 6in..............(2.59m)
Overall height ....3ft 7in................(1.1m)
Ground clearance (nominal) ....0ft 4.5in..........(11.4cm)
Wheelbase................................16ft 0in.............(4.88m)
Track (front)..............................1ft 3in..............(0.38m)
Track (rear)...............................8ft 0in..............(2.44m)
Height of cg above ground......1ft 10.5in..........(0.57m)
Distance between cg and
rear axle..................................8ft 10in.............(2.69m)
Height of roll axis above
ground ....Zero ....Zero

N8 mock-up at DMC's home. (National Motor Museum)

123

Bluebird CN7

the Dawson report, which includes data from wind tunnel tests carried out at Fort Halsted, it seems that the ideal outrigger cross-section was not possible due to the plane area and consequent outrigger size that it would require. Fletcher's calculations showed that the vehicle would be stable aerodynamically up to speeds of over 1000mph (1609kph), but his calculations did not take into account the stability provided by the wheels, so it is clear that CN8 would have been exceedingly stable. The problems of instability caused by the pressure waves at supersonic speeds were not expected to affect CN8 due to the rounded underside of the body being essentially parallel to the ground, the fact that the roll height was at ground level and all points of influence were within the stability triangle of the vehicle. Fletcher also said that: "Its behaviour in the transonic range should be very little different from its behaviour at lower speeds."

Just before this book went to press, I found the accompanying photograph of Ken Norris in a wind tunnel alongside a very advanced design, which looks almost like an aircraft. The wedge projecting from the underside shows that it must have been his latest design for a water speed record hydroplane, and was obviously to be rocket-powered since there's no sign of an air intake. From Ken's appearance he is by then in his late 60s or early 70s (1989-1992) and I suspect it was the design that I had heard of being tested at Southampton University. However, despite numerous telephone calls, I can trace nobody that has any knowledge of these tests. According to one senior lecturer that I spoke to, the data: "Was probably thrown out when there was a major clear-out in the mid 1990s!" Such was the importance of data on what was almost certainly the fastest hydroplane ever designed! Looking at the shape, and remembering how nobody was able, or prepared, to tell me about it, I wonder if another 'D' notice (military secret clampdown) was served on the design, as it looks rather close to the 'Stealth' design of US bombers. It seems a great pity that such an elegant and sophisticated design has not been utilised by subsequent record breakers; but there's still time!

During my research, I found brief reference to another car for which Ken had developed the basic design. He would not have worked on minor improvements, so it would not be unreasonable to expect that its target speed would have been greater than the 825mph (1371kph) of CN8, and most probably 1000mph (1609kph), the speed aimed at for the present 'Bloodhound' project to be driven by Wing Commander Andy Green, some 25-30 years later!

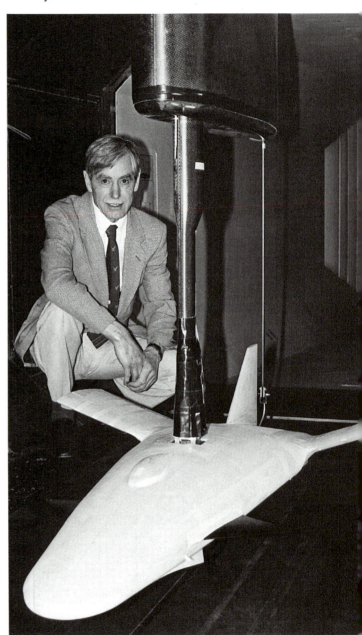

Ken Norris in the wind tunnel with his final design for a hydroplane. (Ken Norris Collection)

What happened to the design team?

Before he died, Ken Norris asked Mike Varndell, with my assistance, to take over a magnum opus that he, Ken, had started on the history of Norris Brothers Ltd. I shall not go into detail on the many other ground-breaking designs that the company produced as that would pre-empt that book, but the following is a list of some of Ken and Lew's company activities in later years. Unfortunately, Ken died in 2005, and Lew in 2009, but were never given any official recognition for their work, which I believe was a grave omission by 'the powers that be' when one looks at the honours granted to so many others for what are lesser achievements.

Ken Norris

Owner of Shoreham Flight Simulation
Owner of A&G Aviation
Owner of Crop Duster Training School at Hern Airport
Owner of Flight of Crop Duster aircraft
Owner of Anglo American Airmotive
Consultant on design of Thrust II and Thrust SSC
Consultant on design of Spirit of Australia
Consultant on original concept of Quicksilver

Lew Norris

Managing Director and shareholder of Worcester
  Valve Co
Owner of Norris Packaging Ltd
Managing Director and shareholder of Worcester
  Controls Ltd
Vice President and shareholder of Worcester
  Controls Inc
Owner of Flotronics Ltd
Owner of Norbro Actuators Ltd
Owner of Process Control Today

Donald Stevens

During my work as Project Co-ordinator for CN7/60 I was in contact with many senior figures throughout British industry, and the company asked me to take on the marketing role which was until then largely carried out by Ken and Lew. Girling approached me to join it as second in charge of its Competitions Department, but my new wife refused to consider a move to the Midlands. A Canadian company had developed a novel filter for removing water from diesel oil for marine engines, which had been adopted by the Royal Canadian Navy and was of interest to the Royal Navy. We obtained European manufacturing rights working through the Commercial Division of the Canadian Embassy in London. I developed a good relationship with the diplomats there and was asked if I would consider joining them to promote Canadian products in the UK. Being newly married and the salary package considerably better than that with Norris Brothers, I accepted.

Bluebird CN7

From late 1963 to 1967 I organised incoming 'missions' of engineering companies, arranged agencies and licensees, and ran large stands at major London trade fairs. At the start of each 'mission' we held a reception for the members to meet influential members of UK companies. At one of these I was convinced by Sir Eric Firth of Firth Brown Ltd in the Vickers Engineering Group, that I should use my talents for Britain, which resulted in him having me appointed as Group Public Relations Manager for one of its companies – Wickman Machine Tools. After my experiences with Jim Phillips at Motor Panels, I should probably have realised that my personality and approach did not fit in with the management style of Midlands companies, and after just over two years fell out with the Managing Director over his cancellation of production of a new optical profile grinder, for which I had lined up both Queens and Design Awards, because: "My friends in industry consider it too expensive." This despite the fact that the existing machine caused major back and neck problems to its highly skilled operators. The crux of our falling out came when I suggested the unions should be brought in to force the idea through. His reaction was: "Mr Stevens, we do not talk to the unions, I suggest that you commence looking for alternative employment." No wonder British manufacturing industry disappeared!

I put the word out that I was looking for a new challenge, and some months later received a call from the Government of Ontario's office in London asking if I would be interested in doing a similar job to that I had done for the Canadian Government, but at a more senior level. That lasted for nearly 10 years until I inadvertently spoiled some very impractical plans of a new Minister of Trade and found myself out of work with no legal recourse due to the fact that it was a foreign government for which I had been working.

By this time I had become involved with yoga, and was teaching it several evenings a week (including at Ontario House) and had developed an interest in natural medicine. Many students were asking if yoga could cure this or that, and I realised that there needed to be a central point which could advise and administer any help required, so I set up a coordinated natural health clinic with eight practitioners, including two doctors, working as a team. It was very successful at cures but not financially, so when I was approached to take charge of an organisation called New Approaches to Cancer, I did so whilst keeping my hand in at reflexology. Unfortunately, we were ahead of our time, and whilst we were wrongly accused of killing people by many cancer specialists, a network of help centres developed throughout the UK. Most of the ideas that we advocated are now part of mainstream advice, and others are being 'discovered' by orthodox medicine. Money ran out, though, and I had to leave, although the organisation still functions – in a limited way, run by volunteers.

For about 10 years then (1982-1993) I kept the wolf from the door by doing freelance public relations work and reflexology. One day I received a phone call from a chap that I had met at a couple of parties and with whom I had had some amicable but strong arguments. He invited me to lunch and asked me to join him to help pull together three rival Southern Water engineering offices and a small consulting engineering company. My title would be Public Relations Manager, but I was to work closely with him to develop UK and overseas markets and to bring the rival offices into a cohesive unit. We did that and I was instrumental in setting up offices in Manila and Zagreb, and developing a nascent one in Dubai. That all came to an end when Southern sold out to Scottish Power who did not want any overseas operations. So, I finally retired from employed work and continued piecemeal work wherever it arose.

Hugh Standing

Hugh joined Norris Brothers in 1956, having started his engineering life in 1941 as an apprentice at the UK branch of Swedish Atlas Diesel AB in Wembley. When his apprenticeship ended in 1945, he was conscripted into the Royal Signals and was posted to Germany as Unit Draughtsman to 53 Div Signals Regiment HQ. A lack of work made him apply to become a vehicle mechanic, which allowed him to continue his interest in engines, and gave him supervisory experience over six German mechanics. He later transferred to the Light Aid Detachment of the Royal Electrical and Mechanical Engineers (REME) on vehicle recovery.

With service completed in 1948 he rejoined Atlas, repairing and assembling its mobile compressors. He then spent two years in the drawing office of Napier Ltd, detailing its world famous 'Deltic' diesel engine. With promotion to the design office blocked, he successfully applied to Porn & Dunwoody, the pre-war agent for Deutz Diesels, as a designer. There he was involved in the mechanical design of a small stationary engine for driving water pumps and generators, which went in to production. With a request to move to a different part of the company – manufacturing lifts – not of interest to him, he moved to the London office of the De Havilland Aircraft Company, working on the design of an infra-red missile guidance system.

Marriage and a house move to Brighton led him to look for work locally, and thus he joined Norris Brothers.

He worked closely with Lew Norris on the mechanical design of CN7, and became famous in the team for being able to remember exact drawing numbers of almost any part of the car. With his 6ft-plus height, big frame, and 'elephantine' memory, Hugh was given the nickname of 'Huge!' He also lead the design team drafted to Harwell for the 'BEPO' Magnox reactor experiment, and developed a patent held by a Commander Chapman that used a novel vibration technique of fuel atomisation in a single cylinder diesel engine. Another of his projects was the design of the jet pump and mechanical systems for the

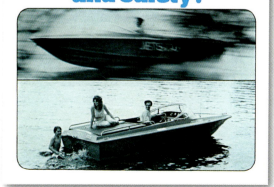

Jetstar advertisement. (Norris Brothers Archive)

What happened to the design team?

water jet runabout/ski-tow, designed for Dowty Marine, the hull of which was designed by Peter Milne, another of the Norris team. (See Dowty note below)

In 1962 Hugh decided that he wanted to work in a more 'hands on' capacity, one that would involve him in development and manufacture rather than the mainly design work at Norris Brothers. He moved to the London office of BTR Oilfield Engineering, developing hydraulic hose fittings and associated products. The office was due to move to a new site in Salisbury, Wiltshire when Hugh's wife died. With two young sons, he decided relocation would cause further upset to them, so he did not transfer to Salisbury after all. The next 20 years up to his 'official' retirement in 1985 were spent at Laser Engineering back in Burgess Hill, designing and developing hydraulic pumps, control valves, and associated products.

His skills were next utilised for another five years at his brother-in-law's company developing quality assurance and control systems for work on electronic components for the European Space Agency, finally retiring in 1993 to enjoy his family, garden and allotment.

Note regarding Dowty Marine runabout:
In 2006 I was made aware that Donald Campbell's personal runabout 'Jetstar' "designed by Donald Campbell and Leo Villa" was coming up for sale at Goodwood. As I knew this claim to be a falsehood I set about alerting the auctioneers, who later came back to me having verified my story! The myth had developed because Dowty Marine stopped producing its water jet pump and another had to be found. DMC was killed just before the redesigned boat was to be launched at the Earls Court Boat Show, and Norris Brothers kindly employed Leo in its development workshop. He did some minor modifications to fit the new pump, and the craft became 'Jetstar.'

Fred Wooding
Fred stayed with Norris Brothers Ltd until he retired. He worked with Ken Norris on concept designs for the dual role record vehicle and the CN8 rocket car. He died in the early 1990s, and, unfortunately, I have to date been unable to trace any further information on him.

Jerzy Orlowski
Jerzy grew up in Poland and was active with the resistance movement against the German occupation. He was captured in the Warsaw Ghetto, but escaped from the forced march taking them to concentration camps. His memories of this time are recorded at the Imperial War Museum.

He worked on a number of projects after CN7, including an automatic gearbox for the National Research Development Corporation. Later he developed an import business for Norris Brothers Ltd with high performance gliders from Poland and pipeline welding jigs and hot water control valves from Germany. When Norris Brothers decided that this business did not fit into its development plans, he left to set up his own company importing and distributing 'Oventrop' radiator valves from Germany.

Jerzy designed the 'Bravamix' water mixing valve for controlling maximum temperature at taps, which became the industry standard for use in hospitals and nursing homes, and was manufactured by Oventrop. His efforts were so successful that Oventrop opened its own UK operation, leaving him as a non-exclusive sales outlet. With friends like that who needs enemies! Jerzy died from a stroke in 1998.

Henry Thwaites

Henry stayed within the Norris group of companies until he retired, eventually running the lift truck manufacturing operation based in Littlehampton, West Sussex. He is still alive at the time of writing, but did not wish to participate in this venture! Of minor interest is the fact that Henry and the author were in the same class at grammar school.

Alan Lucas

I can find no information on Alan's pre- or post-Norris life.

Gordon Dale-Smith

Gordon was educated at Worthing High School, from where he joined the Royal Air Force and trained as an Electrical Technician specialising in aircraft systems. He was posted to 657 AOP Squadron, the army's first helicopter Flight, where he experienced rescue and supply work in the 1953 flooding of the UK's East Coast and Holland, logistic support for troops in West Germany, and the regular transportation of the Chief of the Imperial General Staff (CIGS) Field Marshal Lord Harding on his inspection visits to army camps. His RAF service was completed with No 1 Fighter Squadron at RAF Tangmere, sorting out problems with the then 'state-of-the-art' electronics of the Hawker Hunter fighter aircraft as the squadron's Electrical Section leader.

Back in civilian life Gordon joined Airwork Ltd, an aircraft maintenance company based at the then developing London (Gatwick) Airport, and completed his Higher National Certificate (Electronics) academic training. He joined Norris Brothers Ltd in 1958 and, in addition to his work on CN7, he contributed to other projects, including electrical design work for Redifon Flight Simulators, Harwell Atomic Energy, Woodhall Duckham's Underground Coal Gasification Plant project at Coleshill, and the first piezoelectric ignition lighter for Colibri.

In 1962 he left Norris Brothers to join a subsidiary of ITT in Brighton where he designed transistor circuitry for the first 'electronic' teleprinter, and was promoted to project leader of the design team.

Moving to Motorola in 1966 as a Technical Representative (which, in those days, meant that you had to have indepth knowledge of your products) he transferred to Phoenix, Arizona as Technical Marketing Manager for the UK sales force, promoting Motorola semiconductor devices, mainly to UK computer, industrial and consumer manufacturers, eventually returning to the UK to manage the Defence and Communications Division.

In 1975 Gordon set up his own company, Pelco Electronics Ltd in Brighton, distributing Rockwell International's range of 4- and 8-bit microprocessors, as well as offering hardware and software design and consultancy services, and courses to industry and universities. The company was responsible for the design of a number of 'industry firsts,' including taximeters, and navigation and security systems, amongst other things. A series of buy-outs by ever bigger companies ended in 1982 when Gordon moved out and bought Dolphin Hitec Ltd to design and build microprocessor systems for Initial Services' vending and hand dryer machines, which he ran until 1995 when Initial decided to take over production itself.

Since then Gordon has been designing and operating websites for about 30 golf clubs in the South East of England as well as acting as computer systems consultant. Being a keen golfer this has obviously been 'very hard work!' He is now theoretically retired but still open to offers.

Other designers and draughtsmen who worked on the project are:

Bob Greenaway – designed the canopy and its operating mechanisms.
Dennis Burgess – wind tunnel models and vehicle lines.
Derek Marchant, 'Mac' Macdemitria, RJ Varter, GF Kendall, Stan Taylor, John Turner, E Pinn, Tony Halliday, Colin Abbott, Gordon Sutton, AT Grover, Mike Short, BG Rhead.

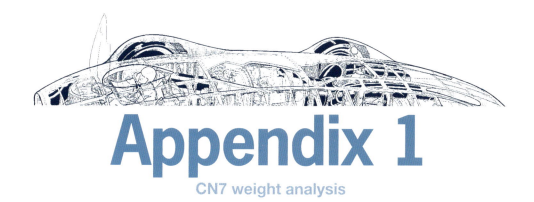

Appendix 1

CN7 weight analysis

Item	Weight	
	(UK lb)	(kg)
Engine	2440	1107
Transmission (gearboxes, shafts, etc)	860	390
Wheels and tyres (including hub assembly and half shafts) ie un-sprung weight	1680	762
Main frame	1600	726
Substructure (including skinning, covers, canopy, etc)	642	283
Mechanical brakes	216	98
Exhaust system	120	54
Steering gear	70	32
Cockpit gear (including driver)	250	113
Controls	30	13
Air brakes and operating gear	130	59
Fuel and lubricating systems (including tanks)	440	199
Radio, recording and breathing equipment	85	38
Instruments	40	18
Suspensions	160	72
Miscellaneous (pipes, batteries, air bottles, jacks, etc)	440	199
Ballast	300	136
Total AUW	9503	4310

Appendix 2

List of 50 companies associated with CN7

Note: Subsidiary companies are listed in pale blue under parent companies.

Acheson Colloids Ltd	Molybdenum disulphate treatment of transmission components
A Macklow Smith Ltd	Load measuring capsules for static tests
Anderton Springs Ltd	Circlips
Andre Rubber Co Ltd	Engine rear eccentric bearer and vibration resistant mountings
Armstrong Patents Co Ltd	'Helicoil' thread inserts
Associated Electrical Industries	Engine booster coils
Automotive Products Ltd	Quick release fastenings
Aviation Developments Ltd	Rivets and riveting equipment
Avica Equipment Ltd	Flexible tubes for oil and fuel supply
BB Chemicals Co Ltd	'Bostick' compounds
Birfield Ltd	Constant velocity couplings
Bluemel Bros Ltd	Steering wheel
Bowden Engineers Ltd	'Bowden' cables
Bristol Siddeley Engines Ltd	Modification and bench testing of Proteus engines. Technical facilities and fabrication of the stainless steel exhaust system
Britax (London) Ltd	Pilots safety harness
British Oxygen Co Ltd	Oxygen and nitrogen supply plus technical assistance
British Petroleum Co Ltd, The	Development and supply of fuels and lubricants, refuelling vehicles, research and survey facilities

British Refrasil Co Ltd	Exhaust insulating blanket
Darchem Engineering Ltd	Stone cladding on exhaust interior (not used)

Appendix 2 List of 50 companies associated with CN7

Broom and Wade Ltd	Pneumatic tools
BSA Co Ltd	Machining high precision components
Burman and Sons Ltd	Design and supply of steering box
CIBA (ARL) Ltd	Assembly and bonding of main beams and other 'sandwich' panels
Coley Metals Ltd	Technical facilities and special metals
Crane Packing Ltd	Mechanical seals
David Brown Industries Ltd	Development and supply of transmission gear boxes
Dowty Group Ltd	
Dowty Hydraulics Ltd	Power jacks and hydraulic power units
Dowty Rotol Ltd	High precision machining of main transmission drive shafts, couplings and components
Dowty Seals Ltd	Moulded rubber components and bonded seals
Dunlop Rubber Co Ltd, The	Development and supply of pneumatic tyres
Dunlop Rim and Wheel Co Ltd	Supply of road wheels
English Electric Co Ltd	Component machining
English Steel Corporation	Half shafts, steel bar and special high tensile steels
Exactor Ltd	Airbrake controls
Ferrodo Ltd	Design, development and supply of brake pads
Girling Brake Co Ltd, The	Development and supply of disc brakes and vehicle suspension system
Henderson Safety Tank Co Ltd	Light alloy fuel and oil tanks
Hertfordshire Rubber Co Ltd	Rubber sheet and sections
Hughes Johnson Stampings Ltd	Supply of precision high tensile steel forgings
Hymatic Engineering Ltd	Solenoid valves
IV Pressure Controllers Ltd	Pressure reducing valves and stop cocks
Joseph Lucas (Electrical) Ltd	Supply of electrical components and assemblies, wiring installation, electric accumulators
King Aircraft Corporation	'Dzus' quick release joint fasteners and filler caps
Light Metal Forgings Ltd	Supply of aluminium alloy forgings
Modern Conveyors Ltd	Fabrication of sub-assemblies
Morfax Ltd	Exhaust extensions
Motor Packing Co Ltd	Gaitors
Normalair Ltd	Pilot's breathing apparatus
Norris Brothers Ltd	Design and project coordination

Bluebird CN7

Owen Organisation, The

Electro-Hydraulics Ltd	Supply and installation of mechanical brake control system, air brake and vehicle hydraulic jacking system
Motor Panels (Coventry) Ltd	Frame and body construction and vehicle assembly
Rubery Owen and Co Ltd	Specialised high tensile nuts and bolts, metallurgical research, and machining of components

Pioneer Oilsealing and Moulding Ltd	O-rings and oil seals
Power Flexible Tubing Co Ltd, The	Flexible metal bellows
Pye Ltd	Micro switches
Pyrene Co Ltd, The	Fire detection and suppression equipment
Ransome and Marles Ltd	Ball and roller bearings and research facilities
Renold Chains Ltd	Sprag clutch, chain and sprockets
Rose Bros (Gainsborough) Ltd	Spherical bearings and rod ends
Rover Company Ltd, The	Development and supply of refuelling and power service vehicles and supply of support cars
Simmonds Accessories Ltd	'Nyloc' nuts and special fixings
Smiths Instuments Ltd	Design, development and supply of all instrument systems, including the illuminated pilot's display panel, technical facilities
SPE Co Ltd, The	Oil pumps
Star Aluminium Co Ltd	Aluminium foil and exhaust insulation
Tecalemit Ltd	Greasing equipment
Thos Firth and John Brown Ltd	Forgings, sheet metal, stainless steel bar and sheet
Tooley Electro-mechanical Ltd	Generators for support equipment
Triplex Safety Glass Co Ltd	Pilot's screen and armoured glass

Tube Investments Ltd

Accles and Pollock Ltd	Fabrication of high tensile steel tubular components
British Aluminium Co Ltd, The	Metallurgical research facilities and supply of all light alloy material for chassis and body construction
Chesterfield Tube Co Ltd	Air bottles
William Mills Ltd	Aluminium castings

United Springs Ltd	Extension and compression springs
Vickers Armstrong (Engineers) Ltd	Wheel hubs, fabrication and machining
WE Sykes Ltd	Precision machining, finishing and barrelling of transmission components
Wildt Mellor Bromley Ltd	Machining high precision components
Worcester Valve Co Ltd	Fuel stop valve

Appendix 3
Copy of CIBA booklet

August, 1960

From : The Technical Service Department

CIBA (A.R.L.) Limited

Duxford · Cambridge · Telephone : Sawston 2121

Technical

Notes 212

Figure 1. The C.N.7 during a trial run at Goodwood. The structure of the car depends largely on adhesives made by CIBA (A.R.L.) Limited.

The "Bluebird" C.N.7

THE "BLUEBIRD" C.N.7

'Aeroweb' Honeycomb Panels in its Structure

NEXT month, at Bonneville Salt Flats, Utah, U.S.A., Mr. Donald Campbell will make a new attempt on the world land speed record. He will do this in a new "Bluebird", the C.N.7 (Campbell Norris, project 7), which has been designed and built over the last five years. The plans and construction are entirely the work of British engineers. The assembly of the car was undertaken by Motor Panels (Coventry) Limited.

The car has been designed to establish a record which will be recognized by the International Automobile Federation. This means that it must have at least four wheels not aligned, always in contact with the ground, with at least two of the wheels steering and at least two driving. This distinguishes the land speed record from the absolute land speed record which could be held by a motor cycle or a vehicle with jet propulsion.

The present I.A.F. record was established in 1947, when the late Mr. John Cobb travelled at 394.196 m.p.h.

The C.N.7 was designed by Norris Bros. Limited, consulting engineers, of which Mr. Campbell is chairman. The power unit is one Bristol-Siddeley

"BLUEBIRD" C.N.7

Overall length	30 ft.
Overall breadth	8 ft.
Overall height	4 ft. 9 in.
Wheelbase	13 ft. 6 in.
Track	5 ft. 6 in.
All up weight	4 tons
Tyres	Dunlop: 52 in. diameter; 8.52 in. section.
Brakes	Girling disc brakes and air brake flaps at each side of vehicle.
Fuel	B.P. "Avtur" 25 gal. total capacity.

Figure 2. A stage in the construction of one of the main beams. One of the skins, one layer of film adhesive and the 'Aeroweb' honeycomb core have been placed in position. The assembly is ready to receive the second layer of adhesive film and the second skin.

2

Proteus 705 engine, developing 4,100 b.h.p. Other main specification figures are given in the accompanying table.

The frame of the car is novel for a land vehicle in that there is great dependence on synthetic resin adhesives. The main beams, auxiliary beams, engine covers, gear box covers, pressure bulkheads and canopy frame were all bonded by CIBA (A.R.L.) Limited, and consist of sandwich panels with aluminium alloy facing sheets and 'Aeroweb' aluminium honeycomb stabilizing cores.

As will be seen in the accompanying drawings, there are two main beams 26 ft. long by 3 ft. maximum height, and four auxiliary angled beams 13 ft. long by 3 ft. maximum height. The facing sheets for all these beams are of 18 swg. alloy with $\frac{3}{4}$ in. of honeycomb core material between. 'Aeroweb' honeycomb material, which is manufactured by CIBA (A.R.L.) Limited, is available in various cell sizes and with

Figure 3. Solid metal inserts are incorporated in the beams at points of attachment of other members.

various foil thicknesses. The type chosen for components in this car has $\frac{1}{4}$-in. cells, and foil 0.002 in. thick. The edges of the panels are sealed with 'Araldite' epoxy resin. The panels which enclose the engine and the two gearboxes on the top and bottom are of similar construction but are curved. One purpose of the bulkhead panels is to sustain a pressure differential of about 3 psi which is expected in the engine bay.

All these panels were made using 'Redux' and 'Hidux' film adhesives in which the bonding agents are incorporated in a glasscloth carrier. In transit, the film is contained between protective sheets of coloured polyethylene film, which are stripped off before the film is used. The bonding takes place in one operation under heat and pressure. As can be seen in the photographs, metal inserts are included in the

3

adhesive in the vicinity of the hot exhaust ducts, 'Hidux', another product of CIBA (A.R.L.) Limited, is used in these situations. 'Redux' adhesive is entirely satisfactory for all purposes up to about 100°C, and has served for many years in many different types of sub-sonic aircraft. 'Hidux', which retains strength up to about 300°C, was developed by CIBA (A.R.L.) primarily for use in supersonic aircraft in structures liable to heating; it was thus a very suitable choice for those panels of the C.N.7 which are expected to become hot.

The canopy frame consists of a curved honeycomb-cored panel, the inner edge of which is filled with 'Araldite' epoxy resin. The edge is tapped to provide a means of attaching the Perspex cover.

As can be seen in figure 11 the frame of the car is of "egg box" construction. It is permanently assembled by riveting, this being reinforced with 'Araldite' bonding.

The adoption of 'Aeroweb' honeycomb panels for several main components of the frame has resulted in very considerable savings in weight without loss of strength and stiffness. During the construction of the car Mr. Campbell said that the concentricity of the main beams was absolutely superb and had greatly facilitated the installation of other components.

core of the panels to take concentrated loads at various points where other components are attached.

To ensure that there shall be no failure of the

Figure 4 (top of page). Two kinds of adhesive film were used—'Redux' film over the greater length of the beam and 'Hidux' film in the vicinity of the hot exhaust ducts.

Figure 5 (right). The two main beams after bonding by CIBA (A.R.L.) Limited.

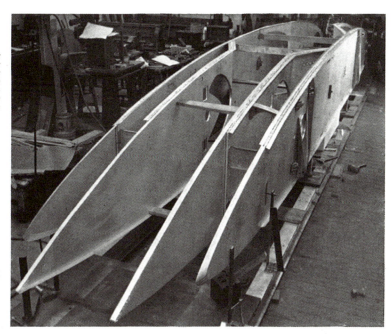

Figure 6 (right). The skeleton of the car at the factory of Motor Panels (Coventry) Limited. The photograph shows in particular the two main beams and two of the four auxiliary beams.

Figure 7 (foot of page). One of the rear auxiliary beams after bonding.

Savings in weight in such a car as this are, of course, of fundamental importance. They not only contribute to acceleration, but in this case were essential to lighten the duty on the tyres. It must not be forgotten, however, that the evolution of a light and powerful gas turbine engine, such as the Proteus, has helped considerably in this direction.

One other point in connection with the use of adhesives in the construction of the car may be mentioned. This concerns the suspension units,

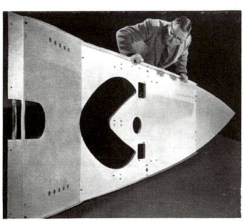

designed in principle by Norris Bros. Limited, and in detail by Girling Limited. They are oleo units, combining spring, damper and rebound buffer. The rebound buffer consists of a conical metal mounting which carries a cylindrical rubber buffer. When the design of this buffer was being considered, it was decided that under full compression the rubber might bulge rather too widely. It was, therefore, decided to divide the buffer into three rings, inserting two metal rings. These were bonded in with 'Redux'. In this way the total bulge of the buffer under compression is restricted, with little loss of total resilience.

It will thus be seen that honeycomb sandwich construction and modern bonding techniques have played a fundamental part in the construction of the C.N.7. It is, however, of interest to give in this bulletin details of some of the other main features of the car.

The Proteus gas turbine engine, giving 4,100 horse power at 11,100 turbine r.p.m. has been modified to drive from both ends, and power is transmitted to the four wheels through two spiral bevel gearboxes with ratios of 3.6 to 1. The driver sits in the nose of the vehicle, forward of the front gearbox. The engine has a ring of air intakes around its centre section. These are fed from the air intake at the front of the car via twin ducts, passing on each side

5

137

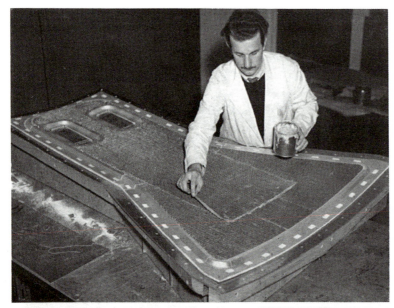

Figure 8 (left). One of the gearbox covers in course of construction.

Figures 9 and 10 (below). The canopy frame is another 'Aeroweb' honeycomb sandwich structure. Being curved, it was bonded in an autoclave.

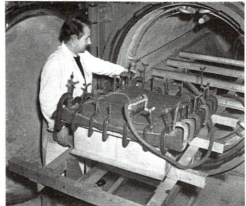

of the driver, and a plenum chamber. The arrangements for exhaust consist of four ducts. Fuel is supplied from two tanks having a total capacity of 25 gallons.

The wheels are sharply dished steel discs, with detachable rims, carrying tyres of 52 in. diameter by 8.5 in. The tyre consists of four layers of rayon cord, with an outer coating of 0.02 in. natural rubber. The cover has to be kept very thin because of the high centrifugal forces which will be exerted at high speed. In the range of 470 to 500 m.p.h., the tread is subject to about 8,000 g. The tyres will be inflated

with nitrogen at a pressure exceeding 100 psi. The inner tube is also of natural rubber, and tyre and tube together weigh 50 lb. The duties imposed on the tyres are extremely exacting, but endurance is not one of the worst, since the duration of a run is only a little more than a minute. The wheels will be changed after each run thus bringing new tyres into use. This has the advantage that it avoids inspection for accidental damage and, in any case, the tyres themselves

Opposite page. In the later stages of design it was decided to make changes in instrumentation and control. The items indicated by red asterisks were therefore not included. Instead there is a system of radio telemetry as described on pages 7 and 8.

6

Figure 11 (*right*). *The "egg box" construction of the car is well seen in this view looking from the front into the air intake.*

Figure 12 (*foot of page*). *Part of the suspension units made by Girling Limited, these rebound buffers incorporate 'Redux' metal-to-rubber bonding, as described on page 5.*

will be too hot to handle immediately after a run. The turning circle of the car is 300 ft., equivalent to a lock of about 5 degrees each way.

The brakes consist of two systems—air brakes to slow the car from peak speed to 400 m.p.h. and disc brakes, acting inboard on either side of the front and rear reduction gears, to bring the car to a halt. The total amount of energy to be dissipated in the 60 seconds of braking is 75 million foot pounds.

The Bonneville Salt Flats provide a course some 15 miles long. Under the regulations, two runs have to be made, one in each direction, the final time being the average. The measured mile has, therefore, to be in the centre of the straightway. There is thus a distance of about seven miles in which the car has to be stopped.

Torque is smoothly transmitted to the wheels throughout the entire speed range without any clutch or gear change. The engine will be started and run up to a predetermined speed, with the car locked on the brakes. Then the brakes will be released and the car will accelerate at a rapid but controlled rate. It will not be possible to apply full torque until the car has reached 200 m.p.h. otherwise there would be drastic wheel spin.

Since it is difficult or impossible at great speeds to watch the road ahead and the instruments, the face

of an accelerometer is being projected on the armoured glass panel in front of the driver, the principle being similar to that of the reflector gun sight. The accelerometer has a scale with two indices, one showing the required and the other the achieved acceleration. A separate panel has conventional instruments needed to check on the serviceability of the car. The driver will wear a mask and breathe air from a bottle, since this reduces problems of ventilating the cock-pit and of misting up.

7

Bluebird CN7

Figures 13 and 14. At trials at Goodwood, Mr. Campbell with Squadron Leader Peter Carr, manager of the C.N.7 project and first reserve driver. Below: Mr. Campbell standing in the cockpit. A cover has been removed to show a wheel and tyre.

A system of radio telemetry is being installed to allow the instruments to be monitored continuously at the base. The driver will be in radio communication with the base, and with the radio telemetry link the support crew will be able to warn the driver should there be an undue rise in temperature of any of the major mechanical components.

Well over fifty firms have contributed components and services to the "Bluebird" C.N.7. The *Financial Times* stated in February that the total development time was likely to exceed 750,000 man hours, at an average cost of 30s. an hour. The final cost, the paper said, was difficult to estimate, but it would certainly run into millions of pounds. The tyre-testing equipment alone had cost £250,000 to develop and produce.

The selection of 'Aeroweb' for such extensive structural use in the "Bluebird" reflects credit upon the enterprise of the designers and upon the reputation of this material, which has been so widely adopted in aircraft and in other structures in which lightness must be combined with high strength.

8

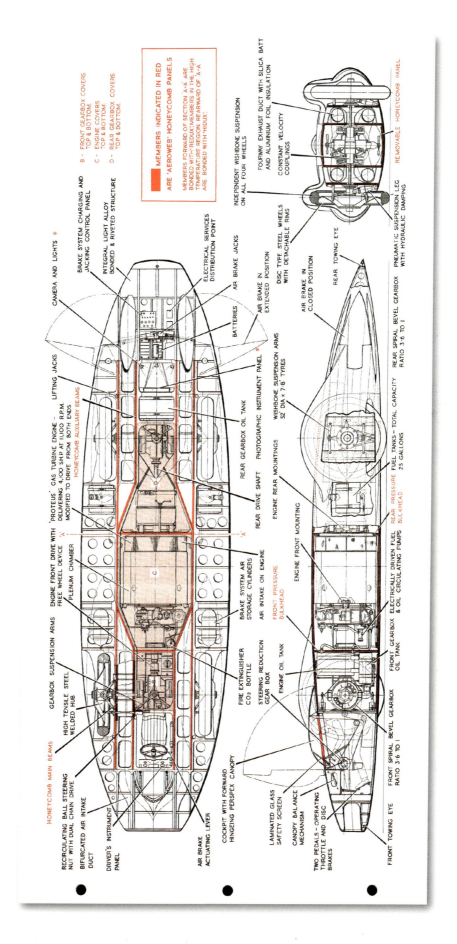

RECIRCULATING BALL STEERING
NUT WITH DUAL CHAIN DRIVE

HONEYCOMB MAIN BEAMS

GEARBOX SUSPENSION ARMS

HIGH TENSILE STEEL
WELDED HUB

BIFURCATED AIR INTAKE
DUCT

DRIVER'S INSTRUMENT
PANEL

AIR BRAKE
ACTUATING LEVER

TWO PEDALS - OPERATING
THROTTLE AND DISC
BRAKES

CANOPY BALANCE
MECHANISM

LAMINATED GLASS
SAFETY SCREEN

COCKPIT WITH FORWARD
HINGEING PERSPEX CANOPY

FIRE EXTINGUISHER
CO₂ BOTTLE

STEERING REDUCTION
GEAR BOX

ENGINE OIL TANK

BRAKE SYSTEM AIR
STORAGE CYLINDERS

AIR INTAKE ON ENGINE

FRONT PRESSURE
BULKHEAD

CAMERA AND LIGHTS *

BRAKE SYSTEM CHARGING AND
JACKING CONTROL PANEL

INTEGRAL LIGHT ALLOY
BONDED & RIVETED STRUCTURE

ELECTRICAL SERVICES
DISTRIBUTION POINT

AIR BRAKE JACKS

BATTERIES

AIR BRAKE IN
EXTENDED POSITION

LIFTING JACKS

ENGINE FRONT DRIVE WITH
FREE WHEEL DEVICE

PLENUM CHAMBER

'PROTEUS' GAS TURBINE ENGINE –
DELIVERING 4,100 SHP AT 11,100 R.P.M.
MODIFIED TO DRIVE FROM BOTH ENDS

HONEYCOMB AUXILIARY BEAMS

REAR GEARBOX OIL TANK

REAR DRIVE SHAFT

PHOTOGRAPHIC INSTRUMENT PANEL *

WISHBONE SUSPENSION ARMS
52 DIA x 7.6 TYRES

ENGINE REAR MOUNTINGS

ENGINE FRONT MOUNTING

AIR BRAKE IN
CLOSED POSITION

DISC TYPE STEEL WHEELS
WITH DETACHABLE RIMS

FRONT SPIRAL BEVEL GEARBOX
RATIO 3.6 TO I

FRONT GEARBOX
OIL TANK

ELECTRICALLY DRIVEN FUEL
& OIL CIRCULATING PUMPS

REAR PRESSURE FUEL TANKS - TOTAL CAPACITY
BULKHEAD   25 GALLONS

REAR SPIRAL BEVEL GEARBOX
RATIO 3.6 TO I

REAR TOWING EYE

PNEUMATIC SUSPENSION LEG
WITH HYDRAULIC DAMPING

FRONT TOWING EYE

MEMBERS INDICATED IN RED
ARE 'AEROWEB' HONEYCOMB PANELS

MEMBERS FORWARD OF SECTION 'A-A' ARE
BONDED WITH 'REDUX'; MEMBERS IN THE HIGH
TEMPERATURE REGION REARWARD OF 'A-A'
ARE BONDED WITH HIDUX.

B - FRONT GEARBOX COVERS
    TOP & BOTTOM.

C - ENGINE COVERS
    TOP & BOTTOM.

D - REAR GEARBOX COVERS
    TOP & BOTTOM.

INDEPENDENT WISHBONE SUSPENSION
ON ALL FOUR WHEELS

FOURWAY EXHAUST DUCT WITH SILICA BATT
AND ALUMINUM FOIL INSULATION

CONSTANT VELOCITY
COUPLINGS

REMOVABLE HONEYCOMB PANEL

(Note: A larger version of this image is printed on the rear endpaper of this book.)

Appendix 4

Copy of Dunlop booklet

NEW PLANT

FOR TESTING TYRES

AT VERY HIGH SPEEDS

The New High Speed Plant.
The position of the underground testing chamber
is marked by its ventilating shafts; the remote control
equipment is in the building above ground.

Dunlop Rubber Co., Ltd.
Fort Dunlop,
Birmingham, 24

An operator at the control desk makes a final check on circumferential speed, using the electronic controls on the left-hand panel, before bringing the tyre into contact with the driving drum. The position of the tyre can be seen on one of the television screens at the centre.

TYRE TESTING
AT VERY HIGH SPEEDS

The Dunlop High - Speed Tyre Testing Machine, modified over the years until it could test tyres at 420 mph, is no longer able to meet the increasing speeds of the World's Land Speed Record. A completely new plant of unique design has recently been constructed and brought into operation. The testing machine itself is contained in an underground chamber and operated by remote control from an adjacent building. A closed-circuit television link enables the tyre to be observed very closely at speeds of 500 mph and more, without any risk.

TYRE REQUIREMENTS AT VERY HIGH SPEEDS

At very high speeds, tyre design presents several special problems. Firstly, the tyre must stand up to the very high centrifugal forces resulting from the speed and when under load at such speeds, it is vital that there should be no generation of 'ripple' or 'standing wave' near the contact area. The tyre must also transmit very high engine power and, equally, transmit high braking torque in the reverse direction.

CENTRIFUGAL EFFECTS

When a tyre rotates, centrifugal forces act in various ways on the different parts of the tyre and, if high enough, will cause disintegration. When travelling at, say 50 miles per hour, the modern tyre can withstand these forces with an ample margin of safety. However, centrifugal forces vary with the square of the speed, so that, other things being equal, at 400 miles an hour (the speed reached by John Cobb in 1947) they are 64 times greater than at 50 miles per hour. At a speed of 500 miles per hour the comparable increase would be 100 times. This basic fact lies behind most of the tyre designer's problems with tyres for very high speeds and, although the effect can be minimised by certain tyre design features, it is still a very big factor.

1

STRENGTH OF MATERIALS

Strength is vital, particularly in regard to the casing material and bead construction. As regards casing fabric, under World's Land Speed Record conditions, the high inflation pressures mean that deflection in the tyre walls is reduced, so that in selecting the textile material, fatigue resistance can be subordinated to absolute tensile strength and low stretch. For this reason, a rayon fabric known as Fortisan is employed, which has extremely high strength and low stretch. However, this particular type of rayon is not necessarily the most suitable kind for ordinary tyres running at normal pressures and is also very costly.

Driving, braking and centrifugal forces are transmitted through the tyre casing to the tyre bead structure and so to the wheels. It is therefore necessary that the beads shall be constructed from a very high tensile steel wire. Special bead spacers are also used, to lock the beads securely against the rim flanges.

RUBBER COMPOUNDS

The treads on very high-speed tyres are unpatterned and only about 1/50th of an inch thick. This is because a thicker tread would be more liable to develop 'ripple' and its extra weight would increase the centrifugal force trying to pull it off; a tread of this thickness provides adequate protection for the casing during at least one run at the record speed. Rubber compounds used for tread, casing and bead construction must be specially designed for low heat generation.

'RIPPLE' OR 'STANDING WAVE'

With 52 inch diameter tyres, such as are being used in the 1960 World's Land Speed Record attempt, a speed of 500 mph corresponds to 50 revolutions per second. Recovery of the deflected casing must therefore be very rapid, if not, a 'standing wave' would appear where the tyre leaves the track. This would cause severe internal stresses and high temperatures, which would result in immediate tyre failure. Tyres for very high speeds must be designed so that no 'standing wave' is generated under the circumstances in which they are used.

To deal with all these problems, the tyre designer has to call for maximum strength in his basic raw materials and make sure that this strength is being used in the most efficient manner. He also has to make the wisest choice when faced with the need to strike a balance between opposing factors.

When he has decided on his approach to these problems and worked out an experimental design for manufacture, he must be able to test the product. To do this he needs a testing machine which reproduces the operating conditions of such events as the World's Land Speed Record. This machine must be capable of being controlled very precisely and must be completely 'under control' at all times, with adequate safety precautions for an emergency. It must also be possible to make accurate records of speeds and temperatures, tyre loading, changes in tyre dimensions, power consumption, and so on, during the course of any test.

THE NEW PLANT

In 1955 serious consideration was given to the requirements for a plant to test tyres at speeds very much higher than the 420 mph of which the existing plant was capable. These reached the stage of a general specification in 1956. Dunlop engineers then began a detailed design study and when this was agreed construction began. The first outward sign of a new plant was seen in January 1958, when excavations commenced for the underground machine chamber.

*The underground machine chamber during construction,
showing its massive walls.*

3

By August 1959, the plant was sufficiently far advanced for calibration trials to begin with existing tyres and, in September 1959, the first prototype of a new World's Land Speed Record Tyre was tested.

TEST MACHINE

This consists of a vertical drum against which the tyre/wheel assembly is pressed horizontally by a hydraulic ram. Under these conditions tests can be made up to 550 mph, but when it is desired to test tyres for resistance to centrifugal forces only, without being loaded against the drum, speeds up to 675 mph can be employed. The load on the tyre can be up to $1\frac{1}{4}$ tons and the machine will take tyres up to 12" wide and 54" in diameter.

A close-up view of the driving drum with a
World's Land Speed Record tyre in position for testing.

Situation   In the event of an emergency at high speed great energies would have to be contained in the machine chamber, so this has been placed underground. A thousand tons of earth were excavated to make room for the reinforced concrete chamber and 350 tons of concrete and $11\frac{1}{2}$ tons of steel were employed in its construction.

4

Bluebird CN7

An underground control room, if situated alongside the machine chamber and constructed so as to allow tests to be directly observed with safety, would be very inefficient because of the extremely restricted visibility. The control room has therefore been constructed above ground to one side and is connected with the machine chamber by closed-circuit television. This makes it possible to watch the tyre safely at the highest speeds. Numerous control mechanisms enable the movements of the testing machine to be controlled very precisely, all the necessary technical information being displayed on a control panel. Calibration grids superimposed on the television image, also enable the tyre dimensions to be measured accurately at the highest speeds.

Drum Drive

The drum is driven by a 450 hp electric motor, the direction of rotation being upwards at the tyre contact area. This is so that the forces applied to the tyre tend to relieve the weight of the three-ton loading carriage, thus helping to reduce friction on its moving parts. Another advantage of this arrangement is that should 'ripple' set in behind the contact area, it can be readily observed without the machine itself obstructing vision.

The drum-drive includes special arrangements for measuring power losses. This is done using photo-electric pulses fed to a phase meter. These pulses also operate an electronic counter, which gives a very accurate measurement of operating speeds. An ordinary speedometer is also fitted, but this is only used to set the speed approximately, final setting always being established from the electronic counters.

Tyre Drive

The tyre/wheel assembly has its own 250 hp electric motor and is also fitted with instruments for measuring power losses. In addition, these instruments are used to measure rotational speeds, braking forces and air drag. The drive shaft includes a Dynamatic brake to impose controlled braking conditions on the tyre. The whole tyre drive unit, which with its base-plate weighs about 12 tons, is connected to the tyre/wheel assembly through a universal joint. At high speeds it is most essential that when the tyre/wheel assembly is moved forward against the drum, the whole drive unit moves with it, so that both are absolutely in line. This is achieved by an automatic electric control.

Braking System

There is more than one braking system on both drum and tyre, each system playing a different part in controlled testing.

The drum is normally brought to rest by a combination of dynamic braking through the driving motor, with disc braking. The disc brake can also be applied with a higher braking effect in case of emergency and is also used for 'parking' purposes. If required, the drum can be brought to rest from 500 mph in 50 seconds.

The tyre is brought to rest by a combination of dynamic and disc

5

braking or by disc braking only, as desired. It can be brought to rest from 500 mph in less than 30 seconds.

*Taking direct readings on a load gauge
in the machine chamber, during calibration
of the loading equipment.*

Tyre Carriage
and Loading
System

It is most important that when the tyre is loaded against the driving drum, the load is known very accurately throughout the test. For this reason there must be an absolute minimum of friction in the loading system. It has therefore been arranged that the three-ton loading carriage floats over its base-plate on an air cushion a few thousandths of an inch thick, which greatly reduces friction. The same principle is used in the Hovercraft.

6

The hydraulic loading cylinder is also specially made to operate with the greatest smoothness, under very fine control.

A further feature of the tyre carriage is the instruments connected with the bearing supports of the tyre/wheel spindle to measure both horizontal and vertical forces, through meter readings in the control room.

Additional
Safety
Features

In addition to the inherent safety of an underground machine operated by remote control, there are numerous other safety devices. For instance, 130 electrical interlocks have to be in the correct position before the machine can be operated and if any of these fail they fail to safety. A tough steel shield is fixed between the driving mechanism and the tyre/wheel/drum assembly, with screens of torpedo netting between the machine and the underground approach passage. Special limit switches ensure that if a tyre deflates it is automatically withdrawn from the driving drum and braked to a standstill. By means of an emergency switch in the control room this withdrawal can be applied immediately by hand, to stop the machine in 60 seconds. Should the machine be brought to rest by any of the automatic safety controls, illuminated indicators in the control room help locate the failure.

CONTROL ROOM

All testing operations are directed from a control desk in the above-ground control room. The design of this desk has been carefully planned, so that two operators have the necessary controls in the most convenient position and at the same time can readily observe all the recording instruments. During short high-speed tests, particularly during braking studies, it may be of value to have a motion picture record of certain instrument readings. These instruments have therefore been grouped on the panels in such a way that they can be picked up by a cine camera without interference from the position of the operators.

The closed-circuit television system operates from two Pye television cameras, mounted on separate pedestals travelling along an optical bench, situated underground just outside the machine room. These cameras watch the tyre through a slit in the machine room wall, one looking at the tyre itself and the other at the wheel shaft or any other part of the equipment desired. Each camera has two lenses, one for a general view and the other for a close-up, brought into use by remote control from the control desk. Both cameras can be moved side-to-side or back-to-front and their movements are recorded in one-thousandths-of-an-inch. In conjunction with the calibration grid electronically superimposed on the television image, this allows for tyre movements to be measured very accurately during testing. Pictures from the two television cameras appear on separate 14" screens forming the central point of the control desk, with the sounds collected by a directional microphone in the machine chamber, coming through a loud-speaker mounted above. The whole effect is as though the operators were actually sitting alongside the test machine throughout the run, with precise measuring instruments ready to hand.

7

The television cubicle alongside the machine chamber. The driving drum and the World's Land Speed Record tyre can be seen through the slot for the cameras

A remotely operated still camera is mounted alongside the television cameras, to provide any record pictures required. Both television cameras and the still camera, with their auxiliary equipment, are contained in a separate cubicle just outside the machine chamber.

HOW HIGH-SPEED TESTS ARE CARRIED OUT

Broadly speaking, four kinds of tests are carried out - Very High Speed Tests - Normal High Speed Tests - Controlled Braking Tests and Spin-up 'Free Fling' Tests.

In Very High Speed Tests the tyre and drum are first run up to the same shaft speed by separate controls, but a most important requirement is that the circumferential speeds are exactly matched before contact is made. For the same shaft speed the circumferential speed of the tyre will be slightly lower than that of the drum, because of its smaller diameter. Final adjustments to circumferential speeds are therefore made very carefully with the aid of the electronic counters and this part of the test may take up to a quarter of an hour. When speeds are exactly matched, the tyre is advanced towards the drum and the tyre drive automatically cut off just before it comes into contact, so from that time onwards the tyre is driven from the drum. When the required load has been applied, running is continued for a specific time, which in the case of World's Land Speed Record tyres is little more than a minute at maximum speed.

Normal High Speed Tests can be carried out in a similar manner, but if desired, the tyre/wheel assembly can be disconnected from its driving system and the stationary tyre brought up to speed by skimming it against the rotating drum, finally applying a specific load.

For Controlled Braking Tests, it is required to imitate conditions during acceleration to high speed and subsequent braking to rest. In this test the tyre is first run against the drum under load at a steady high speed. The Dynamatic brake in the drum-drive is set to apply a specific braking force to the tyre and on bringing it into operation, the drum-drive cuts out automatically. The tyre/drum speed then falls and at a certain speed a different braking force is selected and maintained until the speed falls to a further chosen value, or to rest.

8

With Spin-up 'Free Fling' Tests, the tyre is spun up to whatever speed is required. In these tests the tyre is, of course, out of contact with the drum, the purpose of Free Fling tests being to study reaction to the highest centrifugal forces without normal load application. Measurements can also be made of the power necessary to overcome windage, by means of the torque shaft in the tyre drive.

TESTING PROGRAMME

The Dunlop High-Speed Tyre Testing Plant has been in full operation for the last few months. At the present time its major function is to test the new designs of tyre required for the World's Land Speed Record attempt during the summer of 1960.

The existing World's Land Speed Record stands at just under 400 mph. With speeds of this order, the internal forces in a tyre are of considerable magnitude, so that a relatively small increase in speed means a definite step forward into the unknown. This may call for important changes to the tyre designs which proved satisfactory for the existing World's Land Speed Record. Testing different approaches to solving the problems and, finally confirming a chosen design with repeated testing, entails a very heavy programme of work, so that no other type of high-speed testing is at present being undertaken.

Nevertheless, although the new plant is specially designed for operation at speeds of the order of 500 mph, it can operate with equal facility at lower speeds, that is to say in the 60 - 200 mph range. It will therefore be a valuable tool for proving racing and sprint tyre designs over a very wide field.

The progressive increase in the World's Land Speed Record. It is interesting to see how regularly the speed has increased over the years.

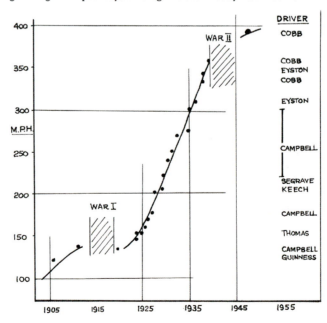

9

Appendix 5

The Land Speed Record since its inception

	Date	Location	Car maker	Car name	Driver
1	17.05.1922	Brooklands	Sunbeam	350hp Sunbeam	K Lee-Guinness
2	06.07.1924	Arpajon	Delage	La Torpile	R Thomas
3	12.07.1924	Arpajon	Fiat	Mephistopheles II	Eldridge
4	25.09.1924	Pendine	Sunbeam	Blue Bird	M Campbell
5	21.07.1025	Pendine	Sunbeam	Blue Bird	M Campbell
6	16.03.1926	Southport	Sunbeam	Tiger	H Seagrave
7	27.04.1926	Pendine	Thomas	Babs	J Parry-Thomas
8	28.04.1926	Pendine	Thomas	Babs	J Parry-Thomas
9	04.02.1927	Pendine	Napier-Campbell	Blue Bird	M Campbell
10	29.03.1927	Daytona	Sunbeam	Sunbeam 1000hp	H Seagrave
11	19.02.1928	Daytona	Napier-Campbell	Blue Bird	M Campbell
12	22.04.1928	Daytona	White Triplex	Spirit of Elkdom	R Keech
13	11.03.1929	Daytona	Irving-Napier	Golden Arrow	H Seagrave
14	05.02.1931	Daytona	Napier-Campbell	Blue Bird	M Campbell
15	24.02.1932	Daytona	Napier-Campbell	Blue Bird	M Campbell
16	22.02.1933	Daytona	Thompso & Taylor	Blue Bird	M Campbell
17	07.03.1935	Daytona	Thompson & Taylor	Blue Bird	M Campbell
18	03.09.1935	Bonneville	Thompson & Taylor	Blue Bird	M Campbell
19	19.11.1937	Bonneville	-- -- -- -- -- --	Thunderbolt	G Easton
20	28.08.1938	Bonneville	-- -- -- -- -- --	Thunderbolt	G Easton
21	15.09.1938	Bonneville	Thompson & Taylor	Railton-Mobil Special	J Cobb
22	16.09.1938	Bonneville	-- -- -- -- -- --	Thunderbolt	G Easton
23	23.08.1939	Bonneville	Thompson & Taylor	Railton-Mobil Special	J Cobb
24	16.09.1947	Bonneville	Thompson & Taylor	Railton-Mobil Special	J Cobb
25	17.07.1964	Lake Eyre	Motor Panels (Coventry)	Bluebird CN7/62	D Campbell
26	02.10.1964	Bonneville	W Arfons	Wingfoot Express	T Green
27	05.10.1964	Bonneville	A Arfons	Green Monster	A Arfons
28	13.10.1964	Bonneville	C Breedlove	Spirit of America	C Breedlove
29	15.10.1964	Bonneville	C Breedlove	Spirit of America	C Breedlove
30	27.10.1964	Bonneville	A Arfons	Green Monster	A Arfons
31	02.11.1965	Bonneville	C Breedlove	Spirit of America Sonic 1	C Breedlove
32	07.11.1965	Bonneville	A Arfons	Green Monster	A Arfons
33	15.11.1965	Bonneville	C Breedlove	Spirit of America Sonic 1	C Breedlove
34	23.10.1970	Bonneville	RDI	Blue Flame	G Gabelich
35	04.10.1983	Black Rock	Thrust Cars	Thrust II	R Noble
36	15.10.1999	Black Rock	G Force/Thrust Cars	Thrust SSC	A Green

(Continues on next page ...)

Bluebird CN7

(... Continued from previous page.)

	Designer	Engine maker	Type	Official Record Speed (mph)	Engine output
1	L Coatalen	Sunbeam	Piston	133.75	360bhp
2	-- -- -- -- -- --	Delage	Piston	143.31	280bhp
3	Fiat	Fiat	Piston	146.01	320bhp
4	L Coatalen	Sunbeam	Piston	146.16	360bhp
5	L Coatalen	Sunbeam	Piston	150.76	360bhp
6	Sunbeam	Sunbeam	Piston	152.33	310bhp
7	J Parry	Thomas Liberty	Piston	169.30	450bhp
8	J Parry	Thomas Liberty	Piston	171.02	450bhp
9	Villiers/Mainia	Napier Lion	Piston	174.88	644bhp
10	L Coatalen	Sunbeam x 2	Piston	203.79	880bhp
11	Vickers/Mainia	Napier Lion	Piston	206.95	943bhp
12	J White	Liberty x 3	Piston	207.55	1308bhp
13	JS Irvine	Napier Lion	Piston	231.44	925bhp
14	R Railton	Napier Lion	Piston	246.09	1320bhp
15	R Railton	Napier Lion	Piston	253.97	1370bhp
16	R Railton	Rolls-Royce R37	Piston	272.46	2260bhp
17	R Railton	Rolls-Royce R37	Piston	276.82	2535bhp
18	R Railton	Rolls-Royce R37	Piston	301.13	2535bhp
19	Easton/Andreu	Rolls-Royce R27 + R25	Piston	312.00	4000bhp
20	Easton/Andreu	Rolls-Royce R27 + R25	Piston	345.50	4800bhp
21	R Railton	Napier Lion x 2	Piston	350.20	2534bhp
22	Easton/Andreu	Rolls-Royce R27 + R25	Piston	357.50	4800bhp
23	R Railton	Napier Lion x 2	Piston	369.70	2534bhp
24	R Railton	Napier Lion x 2	Piston	394.20	2636bhp
25	Norris Brothers Ltd	Bristol-Siddeley	Proteus 425 Gas Turbine	403.10	4310shp
26	W Arfons	Westinghouse J46	Pure Jet	413.10	6200lb
27	A Arfons	General Electric J79 3A	Pure Jet	434.20	15,000lb
28	C Breedlove	General Electric J47/17	Pure Jet	468.72	5700lb
29	C Breedlove	General Electric J47/17	Pure Jet	526.28	5700lb
30	A Arfons	General Electric J79 3A	Pure Jet	536.71	15,000lb
31	C Breedlove	General Electric J79 3A	Pure Jet	555.48	15,000lb
32	A Arfons	General Electric J79 3A	Pure Jet	576.55	15,000lb
33	C Breedlove	General Electric J79 3A	Pure Jet	600.60	15,000lb
34	RDI	RDI hp/LNG	Rocket	622.40	13,000lb
35	Thrust Cars	Rolls-Royce Avon	Pure Jet	633.48	17,000lb
36	Thrust Cars	Rolls-Royce Avon x 2	Pure Jet	763.035	50,000lb

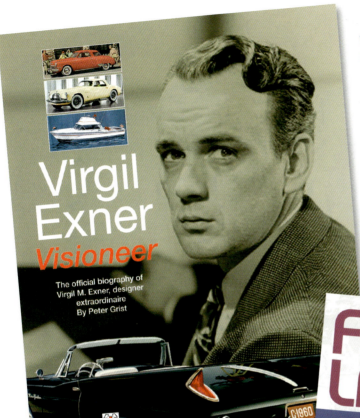

Virgil Exner
Peter Grist

- Hardback • 25x20.7cm • £24.99
- 176 pages • 380 mainly colour photos
- ISBN: 978-1-845841-18-8
- UPC: 6-36847-04118-2

Gets inside the character of the man, his strengths and weaknesses, his personal tragedies and his vision of modern transport. Previously unseen works of art and family photos included. A unique and fascinating insight to a pivotal player in the development of the modern automobile.

Fast Ladies
Jean-François Bouzanquet

- Hardback • 23.9x29cm • £29.99
- 176 pages • 400+ colour and b&w photos
- ISBN: 978-1-84584-225-3
- UPC: 6-36847-04225-7

A veritable saga of female determination to sweep aside male resistance in the inner circles of the motoring world, with a wealth of illustrations spanning almost a century of motor racing. Features over forty unique portraits of some of the daring, brave women who took part in speed records events, rallies and Grand Prix races.

Visit Veloce on the web – www.veloce.co.uk
Details of all books in print • Special offers • New book news • Gift vouchers • Forum
(Prices subject to change • P&P extra)

155

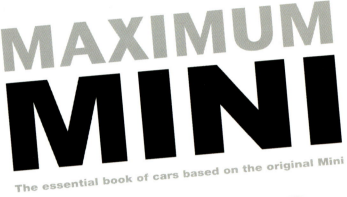

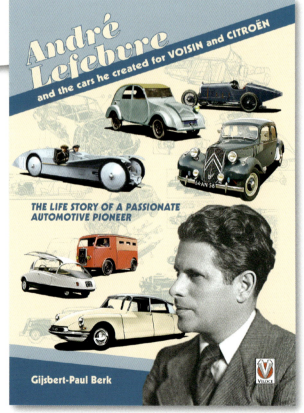

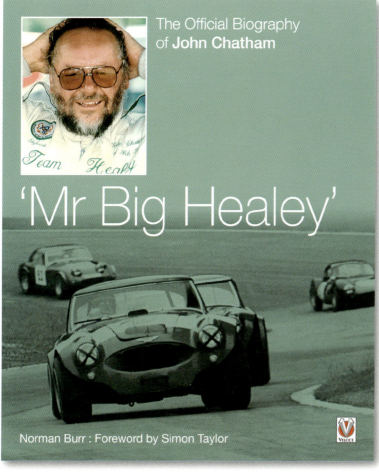

The Official Biography of **John Chatham**

'Mr Big Healey'

Norman Burr : Foreword by Simon Taylor

John Chatham - 'Mr Big Healey'
Norman Burr

• Hardback • 20.7x25cm • £24.99
• 160 pages • 150 photos
• ISBN: 978-1-84584-57-4
• UPC: 6-36847-04257-8

The authorised biography of one of the best-liked 'bad boys' in British motorsport, John Chatham – driver, racer, repairer, rebuilder, tuner, trader and lover of Austin-Healeys. With 150 photographs, many previously unpublished, this is an important and entertaining account of one of motorsport's biggest characters.

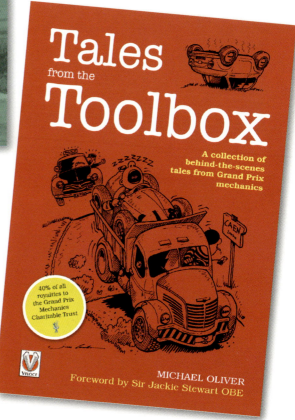

Tales from the Toolbox
Michael Oliver

• Paperback • 14.8x21cm • £12.99
• 176 pages • 50 colour & b&w photos
• ISBN: 978-1-84584-199-7
• UPC: 6-36847-04199-1

A unique collection of behind-the-scenes stories and anecdotes as told by former Grand Prix mechanics who have worked at the top level of the sport during the past fifty years. Supplemented by photographs from the archives and photo albums of the mechanics themselves, this is a fascinating insight into GP racing from a refreshing perspective.

Visit Veloce on the web – www.veloce.co.uk
Details of all books in print • Special offers • New book news • Gift vouchers • Forum
(Prices subject to change • P&P extra)

157

Ford GT
Adrian Streather

- Hardback • 25x25cm • £40.00
- 240 pages • 322 colour & 169 b&w photos
- ISBN: 978-1-845840-54-9
- UPC: 6-36847-04054-3

The complete picture of the Ford GT, including: driver interviews; previously unseen records and pictures; myths and celebrated stories; the GT's opponents on the track; and the GT replica industry. Additionally, as many Ford GT drivers as could be found have been given a place in the author's Roll of Honour. Includes contributions from key individuals.

The Lamborghini Miura Bible
Joe Sackey

- Hardback • 25x25cm • £50.00
- 272 pages • 450 mainly colour photos
- ISBN: 978-1-845841-96-6
- UPC: 6-36847-04196-0

The ONLY book on the Lamborghini Miura to be published in the past twenty-six years! Written by a world-renowned authority on the Miura, and featuring, among other things, a never-before-published factory chassis production register, plus technical illustrations, studio-images, and exclusive interviews with the designers of the car.

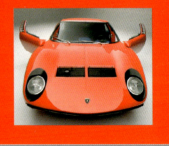

Index

Bluebird CN7

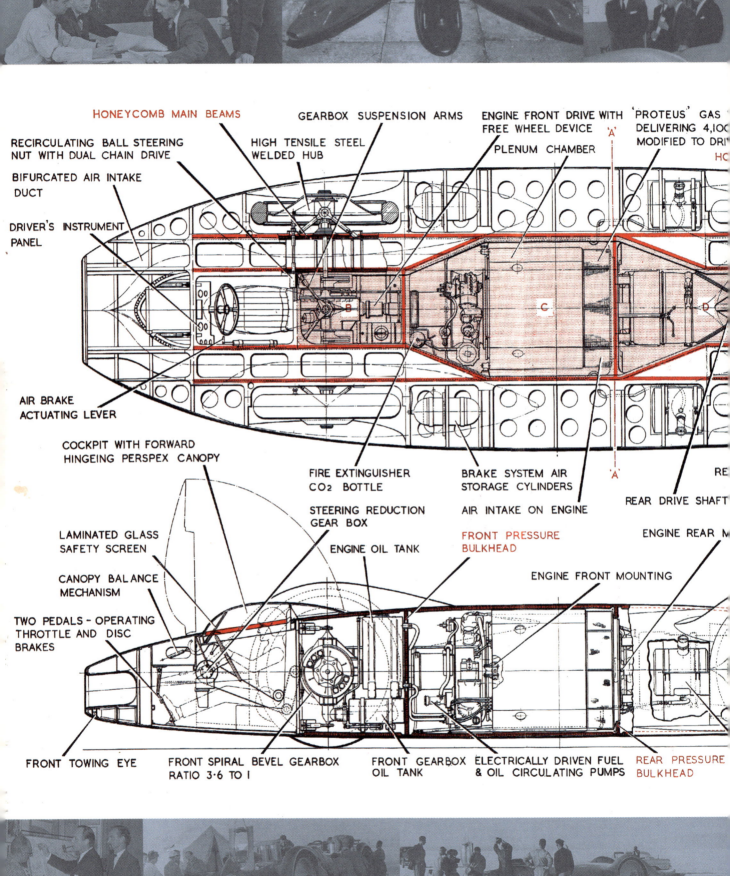

HONEYCOMB MAIN BEAMS

GEARBOX SUSPENSION ARMS

ENGINE FRONT DRIVE WITH
FREE WHEEL DEVICE

'PROTEUS' GAS
DELIVERING 4,100
MODIFIED TO DRI...
HO...

RECIRCULATING BALL STEERING
NUT WITH DUAL CHAIN DRIVE

HIGH TENSILE STEEL
WELDED HUB

PLENUM CHAMBER

'A'

BIFURCATED AIR INTAKE
DUCT

DRIVER'S INSTRUMENT
PANEL

B

C

D

AIR BRAKE
ACTUATING LEVER

COCKPIT WITH FORWARD
HINGEING PERSPEX CANOPY

FIRE EXTINGUISHER
CO$_2$ BOTTLE

BRAKE SYSTEM AIR
STORAGE CYLINDERS

'A'

RE...

AIR INTAKE ON ENGINE

REAR DRIVE SHAFT

STEERING REDUCTION
GEAR BOX

FRONT PRESSURE
BULKHEAD

ENGINE REAR M...

LAMINATED GLASS
SAFETY SCREEN

ENGINE OIL TANK

ENGINE FRONT MOUNTING

CANOPY BALANCE
MECHANISM

TWO PEDALS - OPERATING
THROTTLE AND DISC
BRAKES

FRONT TOWING EYE

FRONT SPIRAL BEVEL GEARBOX
RATIO 3·6 TO I

FRONT GEARBOX
OIL TANK

ELECTRICALLY DRIVEN FUEL
& OIL CIRCULATING PUMPS

REAR PRESSURE
BULKHEAD